MW00534295

Understanding
and Freedom

By the same author

The House I Left Behind

Islam and the Son of God

Christ Above All

The contents of this book are available in DVD
and Audio CD formats. This book contains all
the references for scriptures in DVDs and Audio
CDs. Additionally, it contains supplemental
materials as footnotes.

For more information on Daniel Shayesteh's
books

www.exodusfromdarkness.org

7spirits@gmail.com

Understanding
and Freedom

Detailed Comparison between
Islam and Christianity

By Daniel Shayesteh

Exodus from Darkness, Inc

Copyright © 2016, Exodus from Darkness, Inc.

This book is copyrighted, but may be freely reproduced or distributed in whole or in part as long as this copyright page with the name of the author, Daniel Shayesteh, and of the publisher, Exodus from Darkness, is attached to it. If all or any part of it is used as lecture or teaching material, the credit must be given to the author. In no case, should it be edited or altered in any way.

Author: Daniel Shayesteh, 1954
Understanding and Freedom: Detailed Comparison between Islam and Christianity

Published by Exodus from Darkness, Inc.
York, PA, USA.
ISBN: 978-0-9756017-8-5
www.exodusfromdarkness.org
usa@exodusfromdarkness.org

Contents

Preface

This book brings to light the major beliefs in Islam and compares them with Christianity and other beliefs - information that Muslims desperately need to know. It also reveals how the leaders and teachers of Islam have kept Muslims in darkness, never wanting them to know certain key facts about their beliefs.

The book is a reflection of the things I've become aware of during my own journey from Islam to Christ. Time and again in my journey I was astonished at how and why I was kept in ignorance of Islam's political nature and not allowed to know Islam in the context of the world, and more importantly, to see the beauty in Jesus Christ.

I am so grateful that my life was changed by Jesus Christ, and also, that He has enabled me to share with others about the religious and worldly schemes that can mislead many, including Muslims. My prayer is that the contents of this book become light to millions of Muslims and non-Muslims around the world, and helps them to take shelter in the Prince of Peace, Jesus, in order that they might enjoy a peaceful life, both now and eternally.

Daniel Shayesteh

Introduction

I am going to start a long conversation with you soon through 21 topics. Before stepping into that stage I want to let you know in this introductory section that I have prepared this series in a way to be conversational. Even though I may not be able to hear your voice personally, but I still want to call them conversational since you can allow your conscience to be vocal and get you involved in the evaluation of every issue I raise. Our conversations cannot become meaningful if we disregard our consciences. Therefore, let us promise to each other right from the beginning of this series that we won't ignore the voices of our consciences.

Each topic in this series has a title, but the entire series is named "Understanding and Freedom". I had an amazing encounter with Jesus Christ. He helped me to approach life with understanding, have reason for my belief, avoid blind obedience and live as a free person.

I have spoken to thousands of Muslims, educated and uneducated, tolerant and aggressive, clergies and committed ones personally and also through radio, television and internet in the last decades.

I have seen the huge impact of logical conversation on many of them and how their worldviews changed because of understanding the significance of freedom in every matter of life. These experiences motivated me to prepare these topics and thereby pave the way for you and millions of other Muslims and non-Muslims also to realize how deeply connected understanding and freedom are.

We won't become free either spiritually or socially if we do not look at our beliefs and cultures deeply and find an appropriate way to release ourselves from their dark spots. That's why I have chosen the title of "Understanding and Freedom" for the entire of this series. Understanding and freedom are two very vital and significant needs for our lives. One cannot exist without the other in its real meaning.

Many beliefs and religions keep their followers in ignorance and deprive them of their freedom. It is a fact that their dominance depends on people's lack of understanding and freedom. Any belief that hinders people in comparing their values with others in order to discover the best is a roadblock to people's freedom. Freedom means that nothing has a right to stop you from being clear about things. People who do not have right reasons for having a belief are not free and do not know what real freedom is.

You need to understand that you are responsible to give a solid and logical reason if you claim that your belief is the best and perfect belief. Time and again individuals said to my face boldly that their belief was the best and perfect one. After I asked them to define the words best and perfect for me they then realized that their claims about their belief were not true. That's why I have aimed to help you have reasons for your claims.

After listening to my talks, it will be much easier for you to comprehend that having a belief is not to compete with others or dominate them, but to see whether it values your capability or capacity to discern and decide. A true belief must encourage people to understand things deeply. This is why I was motivated to introduce these 21 diverse topics in order to show a wide range of comparison between Islam and Christianity. I want to prove that understanding is very vital for having a right belief which gives freedom.

One of the greatest obstacles in Islamic countries is the limitation on scrutinizing Islam or comparing it with other beliefs. People do not have freedom to examine their religion. Not only this, Muslims are also forced to speak good about Islam and demonize other non-Islamic values no matter how beneficial and perfect they may be.

Restriction for understanding your belief or others is bondage. If you thirst for freedom, you need to work on your own understanding first, discover the obstacles in your own culture and belief and then find the best way to overcome them. Understanding is a major key for having freedom. Without understanding we will, more likely, suppress our consciences and become blind followers in the service of those who aim to take advantage of our ignorance. For this reason, my first two topics in this series are about personal knowledge and cultural enrichment in order to raise your conscience and create a thirst in you so that you can break chains and become free.

I want to remind you that having the best of everything is your deepest desire and the desire of every other person in the world. Good and healthy things are always for our benefit. That's why we avoid having bad and unhealthy things. This is also true about having a belief or a religion.

We need to have the best belief. Many people have just inherited their beliefs from their parents or communities without knowing whether they are healthy or not. People need to have a belief that gives them confidence, respects their freedom of choice and provides them with a good standard which can help them to have a successful life and peaceful relationships in their families or with others.

To have a beautiful belief like this necessitates zeal, openness, personal initiatives for investigation and comparison, and eventually a courage to make the best decision. Finding a good and healthy belief is not only good and beneficial for us and our families, but it will also shine through us in our communities and enrich our culture. The cultural enrichment in turn makes people prosperous in every way of life and will lead them to discover the most creative principles of life for having a better and more productive life.

We will be deceived by opportunists and become preys to their unhealthy plans in every aspect of life if we do not use our brains, hearts and consciences. I have raised many issues in my talks so that you can understand that the lack of

13

knowledge can trap us in many ways. But knowing the truth will set us free.

I have put the topics, more or less, in order and in a way so that the result in one will help you to understand the following topics better. The first two topics will help you to value understanding. They are also there to remind you that you are capable and have capacity to evaluate everything and make appropriate decisions personally. Following these two topics, İ have given examples of my life to show you how others approached me and helped me to use my brain, heart and conscience and gain back my God-given freedom which opportunists had violated because of my ignorance. As others helped me, I also need to help you gain your freedom too so that you also can help others to become free. Freedom is good for everybody. Each of us needs to be a messenger for freedom.

Following my examples, I have spoken about God through fives topics in a comparative way so that you do not miss anything about God. The word God is taken as the root in your religion or in any other religion. You need to know on what root you are established. By understanding the root of your religion you will then decide whether to keep your religion or leave it and find a better one. We are created in a way to choose the best one.

I will bring everything about God to the surface for you to understand whether God exists or not. If He exists, whether He hides himself from you or reveals Himself to you. You will also learn how to distinguish the true God from the false; whether the god of your religion is a good guide to you or you need to search for the true God.

Through the remaining topics I have shown the philosophical, doctrinal and all other ethical inconsistencies that a false image of God in a religion can create in a society and ruin life in many ways. As I reveal the problems, I speak about the best solution too. I have tried my best to help you get rid of problems, overcome ambiguities of your belief and live as a free person.

My sincere advice to you is to value your God-given identity, get your mind, heart and conscience to work in everything you hear from me, do not allow any preconception to hinder you from listening to all my talks. I promise you that listening to them carefully will be for your benefit and for the benefit of all - Muslims or non-Muslims.

Thank you so much for being ready to walk with me through this series.

Daniel Shayesteh

January 2016

Why Do We Need Personal Knowledge?

Personal knowledge about what we believe or what others believe. All need to know that life does not function well without understanding and reason.

Without knowledge we'll be left behind

Knowledge is like a light to our life. We need knowledge for everything in life; for buying food, clothes, a house, cars, for finding a spouse, friends, raising our family, for accepting or rejecting beliefs, values and every other thing. Imagine if we closed our eyes to choose things, partners or friends without knowing their qualities or personalities. What would the result be? Therefore, it is so vital to choose with open eyes the values that can make our political, social and economic relationships peaceful, joyful and meaningful.

To have a right belief requires knowledge

If we don't know the right way, we won't be able to reach our destination. With the same logic, if we do not know the right belief, we'll be lost spiritually and unable to unite with God.

Life without knowledge is a total loss

An unwise man wanted to build a house, but he did not know that a house had to be built on a solid foundation. So, he built it on sand. When a flood came, the house collapsed. If he had had knowledge, he would have built his house in a place where it would be resistant to a flood. Therefore, as air is vital for living, knowledge is also vital for finding a good belief. Real life should be a searching process for the best option to fulfill our needs. We cannot have the best future if we do not discover the best belief for our life. Searching is a God-given gift for everybody. Investigation must be a part of our belief. We should not follow beliefs that are closed to personal investigation and do not allow people to choose their desired beliefs.

For decision-making we need knowledge

We need knowledge to make appropriate decisions personally, and as the members of a family or a community. As our decisions affect our own individual lives, they will also affect our

18

family and community lives through our relationships. Therefore, a decision with knowledge will be good and productive for everybody. But a decision without knowledge will be less productive or even harmful for all, especially when it is made by leaders, either in a family or in a business or in a nation. You are a leader or are going to be a leader sooner or later. You therefore need to have sufficient knowledge for appropriate decision-making for having a successful personal or family life. So, knowledge is vital for everything.

What steps do we need to take in order to advance our personal knowledge?

I am going to give you ten interdependent steps for gaining knowledge.

The first step is that we must have our eyes and ears open

Eyes are for seeing and ears for hearing. Those who close their eyes and ears to this simple philosophy or block the path for others to see and hear, degrade themselves and others against God and humanity. The eyes and ears of the true God are always open; humanity needs to follow the same principle for truthful living. Life will be more productive if we use our eyes, ears, minds and hearts for learning. A truth-loving person needs to look into other beliefs, listen to their messages, compare them with one another and with his own belief, choose the best for himself, and then live with its logic. Any person or belief that hinders you from searching for truth cannot be truth-loving or promote love.

The second step is that we must discover the obstacles and solutions

What are the obstacles to your learning? Is your belief the obstacle? Are you the obstacle? Is your family the obstacle? Are the social and political problems in your society the obstacles? Is your government or leader the obstacle?

No matter what the obstacles may be, they are against you, your family, country and even the world. You need to discover them and find the best way to rescue yourself from their effects.

The third step is that we need to get our consciences to work

Conscience is an amazing agent in you for confirming and speaking truth. You should not suppress your conscience nor quiet it. A person is dead spiritually if his or her conscience does not have a voice. A free conscience accepts the correctness of another person who is correct, even if you do not like him. Those who ignore the rights of others are those who ignore the voices of their own consciences. Those who reject the best advice and way of life are those who reject the importance and credibility of their own consciences. He who ignores his own conscience will not be able to respect the rights of others. A free conscience does not allow us to belittle the rights and freedom of others, even if they are our opponents or enemies. A free conscience teaches us that there is no difference between a king and a beggar, a leader and a follower, a master and a slave, a husband and a wife; all are human and have the right for freedom. Therefore, you need to stay away from everything, including your belief, that limits your conscience.

The fourth step is that we need to search for the best with thirst

We will not receive water if we do not express our thirst. Knowledge for the best values also will not be gained without thirst and initiative.

Are you longing for the best and most fruitful way of life? If yes, you then need to search for it with thirst. It is the thirst for understanding and discovering that will reveal the truth to us and thereby free us from false beliefs.

The fifth step is that we need to practice freedom personally

People are created for freedom; otherwise, they will fall behind in every area of life. We need to have individual freedom and autonomy in searching for truth. Since we are individually responsible to live and demonstrate the truth via our own life, we therefore need to discover the truth with our own autonomy too. In other words, truth won't make sense for us if we do not have autonomy. A person will not be able to use his or her full capacity in search of truth without autonomy and freedom. On the other hand, if you are not able to search for truth with your full capacity, you won't be able to have the whole truth. For this reason, if anything in your society, including your belief, is limiting your God-given freedom and capacity in searching for truth, you need to find the best way to break that chain and free yourself. The practice of autonomy in investigation will bring accurate knowledge into your life, and that knowledge will open the door to you for a successful life.

The sixth step is that we need to follow a belief open to freedom

No matter how wonderful your parents or forefathers were or are, they can give a belief which can block the way of your success. You need to replace that belief with a belief that opens the door of success to you and to your community. No matter how compelled you are in following your religion or belief, if it is against your freedom and autonomy, you need to replace that religion or belief with something better. All individual, family, social, political, economic and moral improvements in developed countries are because of the courage of those men and women who dared to follow the values of a belief open to freedom. Not only did they advance, but also opened the door for the advancement of others. Because they followed a belief which taught them that the advancement of others will bring advancement for themselves as well. So, once again, if you have a closed belief, you need to leave it and follow a belief that is open to freedom.

I want to tell you with all honesty that if you follow a belief that respects your freedom and everyone else's, you will be released from the agony of a restrictive culture. Truth will set you free.

The seventh step is that we need to be courageous

We, as individuals, need to take initiatives for our own advancement. If I, as an individual, desire advancement, I need to take the necessary steps for my own success. A personal desire for truth should create strength and thereby overcome obstacles. Courageous people can find a way out for themselves or for their family members even when surrounded by many kinds of external pressures. Courageous people are able to step out of the circle of their closed beliefs and search for the best values. Be courageous.

The eighth step is that we need to pay the price

We need to pay the price for obtaining and advancing our knowledge. We need to invest time and maybe money. Sometimes, the price for gaining necessary knowledge is higher than our expectations. We need to be ready for that too. We need to be ready for the attacks of narrow-minded and superstitious people or dictators who build their interest in the ignorance of others. All of these sacrifices will be for our benefit and for the benefit of our families, societies and the world.

The ninth step is that we need to make victory our personal goal

There is no obstacle without a solution. You need to become victorious over every obstacle in life, including your belief, which aims to keep you uninformed. The most practical way to overcome the obstacles of life is to discover the best belief or way of life and make it your own. Yes, you need to find the best belief. Humanity is created capable of searching and finding the best for him or herself, the best belief that gives victory over obstacles. Victory over all obstacles will be yours if you aim to have it.

The tenth step is that we need to wake up our societies

Nothing but our knowledge of truth and zeal for more understanding can wake up our societies. In every possible way, we have to shine as lights of truth, paving the way for others to learn from our experiences and to shine among others. If you are alone, you have to work hard to make friends who are also searching for truth and grow in companionship so that many are awakened and freed. Also, we need to build our relationship stronger with those who have the same mission as we do until all enjoy freedom.

Our awareness depends on our own choices

No one can force us to change and be aware of things unless we ourselves decide to change. If the entire armies of the world gather together and force us to wake up to the truth, we will still not be awakened truly unless there is a real desire in us. Even if the loveliest and kindest person in the world makes his way up to become our government leader, he will not be able to lead us to truth unless we desire to break the shields in our hearts and pay attention. To wake up and change is up to each of us as individuals. We need to decide to change. Let us start with our self, step into the true life and be renewed. Practice matters.

Conclusion

If you believe in God, you need to know that the true God desires people to have knowledge. God is all-knowing and knows what true and false and the best and worst are. For this reason, God desires people to know the difference between truth and falsehood, and to choose the truth.

God is free Himself and desires everybody to be free. God is perfect and he wants us to reside in perfection. Therefore, any belief that limits our freedom, knowledge or improvement is not from God.

The first person to become free is you

The first person who needs to run to freeing belief and become free is You. Please don't say, "no one is interested in practicing freedom, how can I then practice it?" You need to approach freedom in this way and say: "If freedom is the best, is there any reason for me to avoid it?" Then the response will be "No. I have to practice freedom.

I need to follow a belief which values my freedom, opens the door of knowledge and truth for me."

Improvement becomes the catalyst for further advancement

The door of change and improvement will be open to our families and friends if we decide to change and improve. Because of us, they will also be the hands and feet for the knowledge and improvement of others. When we become the cause of change and improvement for people around us, we will advance with them in the pursuit of our own goals. That's why it is so important for us to work hard so that people in our society understand that the freedom of investigation, writing, speaking and belief are the rights of all, stand for their rights, and if necessary, pay the price for the rights of people. Every child in our society needs to learn why we have an obligation to stay away from outrageous beliefs and follow a belief that teaches freedom, kindness and peace.

There will not be a place for dictatorship in a free society

A society that has gained knowledge and freedom will no longer have a place for dictatorship. It is for this reason that dictators block the road to comparative knowledge so that they can rule. Dictatorship and knowledge do not go hand-in-hand.

Knowledge of truth makes lives and relationships fruitful and beautiful in family and society.

Reflection Time 1

1. Give some reasons why people are hindered from having knowledge of their own and other beliefs.
2. Are there ways whereby we can encourage people to be open minded and compare their beliefs with those of others and choose the best? What are they?
3. Does our lack of knowledge about the truth make God irrelevant in our lives? How?
4. What are the benefits of understanding?
5. If understanding is good, is there any reason for us to neglect it?

The Need to Erich Our Culture. Why? How?

What is culture and where does it need enrichment?

Culture involves beliefs, values, languages, customs, idioms, ethics, behaviors, music; and in short, forms the identity of a nation.

So you see that it is the components of a culture that make it spotted or spotless. As a result, enrichment also must take place among the components in order to make the culture a quality culture. To have a good quality culture does not necessarily mean that you need to get rid of your present culture, but to enrich or replace the parts which have become blemished. For this reason, you need to open your heart to the best values of life, even if they are from those people whom you do not like. Because good values are always good, no matter where they come from, they are there for everybody. We need to delightfully replace the darker components of our culture with these good values in order to make our culture beautiful.

Have you thought deeply about your culture? Allow me to share with you some problems that blemish the components of a culture. Maybe your culture is blemished and needs restoration.

Meddling problem in a blemished culture

Isn't intruding in the lives of others and ignoring their autonomy a daily habit in Islamic culture? Because of the authoritarian nature of Islam, all who are older than you in your extended family meddle in your life even though you are mature and have your own family. Government and sometimes people too do not respect your freedom. Your own family and extended family members also become harsh to you if you do not think or believe like them.

Such inappropriate interferences are always the causes of insecurity among family members, in the society and are road blocks to improvements in every way. Why? Because people hesitate to bring newness into their lives in order to keep their relatives or leaders happy and avoid more disruptions. The society remains closed to new and good things because of harsh relationships.

Disrespect towards critics

Life in a culture where criticism is not tolerated becomes extremely harsh. Many people do not treat their free thinking fellow citizens with dignity because of fear from leaders. They are expected to stay away from critics or opponents. The reactions may become very violent if the critics are women or girls. Criticism of political leadership is very costly, and the criticism of someone with a higher rank may also cost a great deal.

In such an intolerant culture, people will choose silence over injustice and progressively fall into the hands of further injustice. Injustice also will in turn stifle creativity, increase indifference, intolerance and hostility and block the way of progress.

Tell me honestly, is your society struggling with this kind of darkness? If yes, then you need to search for light outside of your culture and to fulfill your responsibility in restoring your culture.

Fear from insiders

Time and again we have witnessed many Muslims thinking and acting secretly. They don't want their own family members or fellow Muslims to know of their decisions. They have greater trust in those outsiders who respect freedom of choice, but they hardly trust their own people since there is no respect for freedom among them.

This fear is the result of such abnormal interference among Muslims which has created distrust and disharmony. No society can grow in fear, distrust and disharmony.

Has your society created such a fear? You need to unchain yourself from this fear and not let anyone put you and your dignity down. My teaching is to help you to preserve your dignity and also teach others to do likewise.

Concealing the dark spots of culture

Some tend to justify or conceal the unjustifiable, or deny its existence. For example: There is a religious permission in Islam for Muslim men to beat their wives, yet Muslims refuse to confirm this to outsiders. Or, Islam gives permission to lie under some circumstances but Muslims deny it in front of strangers.

Such suppressive values will remain in a culture and create much loss unless revealed and challenged. The best way to enrich your culture is to reveal its darker parts so others can see and offer you better options.

Exaggeration and twisting the truth

Does your culture focus greater attention towards presenting a superficial appearance, introducing failure as victory or exaggerating small victories? Have you tried to stay away from this darkness? If not, then you need to adopt good values from a good culture and renew your culture in these areas and free yourself and your family from such darkness.

You were taught from childhood that you have to keep your appearance pleasant but hide the unpleasant things inside you. This teaching is not honest. If you keep the darkness inside you, your entire life will be affected by darkness, and you will not be able to have a long lasting happiness but only a superficial one. You need desperately to cure your tongue and your culture from such a damaging darkness.

Favoritism

Some people shelter favoritism and partiality, which is not in the best interests of society. Favoritism opens the door to lawlessness, discrimination and chaos. And favoritism in a society can degrade a culture more when someone with inexperience gets promoted in place of experienced, more qualified worker. Favoritism also opens the door to people who are unfit for leadership, further jeopardizing the culture.

If your belief allows favoritism, you need to adopt a belief that rejects this darkness and leaves the door open to a better life.

Generating irresponsibility

In some beliefs, people are encouraged to turn to the wealth of others instead of working hard and relying on their own income. One of those beliefs is Islam that teaches its followers to loot others who are not Muslims. With such a belief that dishonors others, you cannot have a good culture.

You need to replace it with a belief that appreciates hard-working people, including strangers, and respects the right of all. A good culture or belief must teach responsibility to its people against laziness, so that they can stand on their own feet and become productive citizens instead of taking others' belongings.

Extreme nationalism

An extreme nationalist is someone who says: "Our people are better than others. We do not need to change. We are open only to those who think like us. Strangers are strangers. We have to dominate others."

This is not a healthy nationalism. A healthy nationalism is one that values and upholds not only its own culture, but also reflects an openness and curiosity towards that of others. Nationalism that promotes segregation creates a stagnant culture.

Uncertainty in culture

There is uncertainty in many aspects of life within some cultures. A great cause of this uncertainty is the dominant belief that fosters ambiguity about the future instead of assurance. Such doubt will penetrate into every part of life, including social and political relationships, and may create distrust among people.

Uncertainty is a spiritual darkness that leads into all manner of darkness, if not cured. In an uncertain culture, the courage to break faulty traditions of ancestors decreases. Criticism is not tolerated, and to express a desire for newness is costly. Everyone is forced to speak well of their beliefs and authorities and keep quiet about wrong instructions or actions. Generally speaking, people are forced to accept everything leaders impose on them.

A good example of this uncertainty and ambiguity can be found in Islamic countries where even in a group, leaders distrust their companions and vice versa. Sometimes an individual is humiliated, imprisoned or even killed by a family or a group member for the cause of religion or politics.

The tension between Sunni and Shia started 1400 years ago in a similar way among the successors of Muhammad. This took place after his death and remains the same to this day.

You see how uncertainty in a belief creates uncertainty in relationships which promotes dishonest tactics and self-seeking culture. There is a saying among Iranians, which says: 'even a dog doesn't recognize its master', referring to that uncertainty. It is hard to beat the confidence of a dog in its master. But if the master is uncertain, that's what makes the dog lost and wandering.

In an uncertain culture trust is very rare and has many conditions attached to it. Harmony is not deep but superficial and accompanied by much lip service. Although people desire better relationships, there are many invisible walls which hinder harmony because of the uncertainty in their culture. Because of this disharmony, the rights of others carry a secondary importance and are ignored easily. Friendships are normally temporary and can turn into hatred by anything, small or big.

Does your culture have the above mentioned problems?

If yes, then do your part to change it. How?

You need to start within your own context

Stay away from the things that corrupt your life and culture. If your belief or religion has negatively impacted your culture, act on it; find out why and search for a belief that promotes freedom, peace and has respect for all, friends and strangers alike. Choosing not to act can be detrimental to society.

The effects of bad things are always detrimental

No wisdom in the world so far has endorsed bad things as beneficial. Harmful aspects of a culture are damaging. You each have personal and social responsibility to stay away from engaging in them. Adopt good things from other cultures and put them into practice in your own life and be renewed. Your new life will be a light to your culture and society. Many others will learn from you, do the same and make a positive impact on your culture.

Never, never turn back from your responsibility in contributing good things to your culture

Let me give you an example of indifference so you can see how dangerous it can be for you and others.

A German pastor, Martin Niemöller[1], describes how indifference in him impacted his and others' lives negatively. He said while Hitler was killing communists, he said to himself that he was not a communist and did not need to defend them. He had the same excuse when Hitler killed Jews and others. After Hitler finished killing others, he started to get rid of insider opposition too. It was then that Martin was jailed also. He said no courageous people were left any more to defend him against Hitler. If he and people like him had defended the lives of people who were slaughtered before, now he would have many people in his society to defend his own life.

A passive stance is a cultural darkness which leaves room for wrong to flourish until all of society is harmed. That is why you need to enrich your culture. Culture is not static but dynamic and changeable. We can improve our culture by embracing wholesome values that reject darkness. There is a responsibility on your shoulder to enrich your personal and national culture.

---

[1] https://en.wikipedia.org/wiki/First_they_came_...

Reflection Time 2

1. In a world with diverse beliefs and opposing values, what is the best approach for peace and harmony?
2. Why does the enrichment of our culture matter?
3. Where do we start enriching our culture?
4. Is there any connection between courage, cultural enrichment and advancement?
5. Do you have a responsibility to enrich your culture?

Examples of Personal Change from Daniel's Life

I have an amazing experiences to tell. I have started these series of talks to tell you that understanding is the key for our freedom. We need personal knowledge about everything, including our beliefs, not only to protect ourselves from false beliefs, it is also necessary to improve in the pursuit of our life goals with the best values. I also told you that we have a great responsibility on our shoulders to enrich our culture if we desire to have freedom, be creative and advance in our relationships in our homes and societies.

It would be hypocritical and deceitful if I myself have not experienced such a change, but ask others to open themselves to changes. For this reason, I have chosen to speak about the personal changes in my own life in this part of my talks so that you can understand that my talks are the reflections of the good changes in my own life. I have a true story to tell. I am changed, renewed in mind and heart and have been blessed by the changes in my life abundantly. I wish you to weigh my reasons, consider such newness and be blessed too.

Jesus taught me that if I myself was not renewed first, my expectation from others to change would be meaningless. Before I call others to pay attention to good things, they first must grab my own attention. If a peaceful, kind and loving relationship does not capture my whole being, if patience and forgiveness become just mere words for me and do not play significant roles in my daily life, if justice is only good when others follow it, then all my story, talks and advice will be unproductive and in vain.

I grew up in an environment which valued superficiality more than truth. People normally expected others to change but not themselves. I was, therefore, doing things which would make me very angry if others did those things to me. Such attitudes are the echoes of a self-centered life which sees the rights of others insignificant. Jesus Christ teaches if the lives of others do not matter for you, if you are not in pain for the pains of others, your talks and teachings will be irrelevant to them.

The work and leadership of Jesus Christ in my life was and is to sift the words and attitudes through the sieve of my conscience and keep those that shape my identity for good, but throw out those which chain me to indifference, ignorance, disrespect, discrimination, hatred or war.

One day I saw a television advertisement in a country which was to encourage citizens to avoid dropping litter in streets and keep their city and environment clean. Then people could enjoy the tidiness in their city. In the advertisement a lady had parked her car on a street, was pealing a mandarin and throwing the skins in the street. A man who was passing by collected the skins and threw them back into her car. She got angry at him for making her car dirty. His response to her was that he just did to her exactly what she was doing to others and that she had no right to become angry if her actions were good.

That was a good and educational advertisement. It showed that she was unable to see her conscience, to see a big problem with her own attitudes, making the city of millions dirty, but was very quick to get angry when somebody else did the same to her and made her car dirty. She needed someone to wake her up so that she would be able to refer to her conscience and see the serious problem of self-centeredness in herself and, as a result, find an alternative solution for having peace with others.

Conscience is one of the greatest blessings we, as humankind, have inside us to get us to think, weigh things around us and stand for the best. Believe me if there was not a conscience in us, I wouldn't want to have this conversation with you. Because it would be hard for us both to understand each other without a conscience. Fortunately, we have this conscience and because of it I am so heartened to talk to you, tell my story and share my heart and knowledge with you with the hope that they can reveal the keys for newness.

I have learned from the Gospel of Jesus Christ that I have to rely on my conscience and encourage others to do the same, otherwise we may act as a barrier to the truth. This is what the Gospel says in the book of 2 Corinthians chapter 4 verse 2: We have renounced the hidden things of dishonesty, not walking in craftiness, nor handling the word of God deceitfully; but by manifesting of the truth commending ourselves to every man's conscience in the sight of God. (KJV)

The Gospel is right. The truth does not need dishonesty and craftiness. The truth speaks to the minds, hearts and consciences of people and is able to prove its truthfulness. The truth never uses dishonesty and deceit as bridges to get into people's lives.

In the light of this great wisdom of Jesus Christ I also believe that your conscience has made you capable of weighing things and discovering whether they are truthful or not. Your heart and mind may go for untruthful things but your conscience does not. For this reason, I want to convey my story, my experiences, my knowledge and understanding to your conscience. I hope and pray that you allow your conscience to be vocal and guide you to a right decision.

The changes in my life have happened from the root to the branches. I learned an amazing wisdom from the Gospel of Jesus Christ. It says in Romans chapter 11 verse 16: if the root is holy, so are the branches. (ESV) It brings forth the meaning that everything in our physical and spiritual life depends on the root we have. Our life is the reflection of the foundation or the root on which we are established. If our root or foundation is good, our life will also be good. Otherwise, we will not have a good life.

Therefore, it is very vital for us to choose a truthful foundation or root in order to be established on that root and live with the truthful nutrition it supplies. But the truth is that we won't be able to have a truthful root unless we have a truthful belief. Only a truthful belief can give us a truthful root.

That root is God or the leader who has authored your belief. That's why I needed to find the true God or leader and establish myself on His values. A God or leader that would respect my freedom of choice and teach me to respect the freedom of all, both family members and others. This leader is the God that Jesus revealed to me. Not only does He respect people's freedom of choice but also desires to have a personal relationship with people in order to reveal all good things to them personally. Unlike the god in Islam, He does not hide himself from people who desire to have Him. He has created us personally for a personal relationship with Him.

Isn't it good and amazing to have a personal relationship with God, with the One who has given you life and is the source of every good thing? Of course it is. That's why I have an amazing story to tell you and the world. To tell you what happened and why I have a personal relationship with God.

You see, I am using the words "what and why". I love the words "why, what and how?" I learned from Jesus that these words are very important words of life. These words rescue us from untruth, fear and blind obedience, but establish us on truth, courage and willful decision-making. You are not allowed to use the words "why, what and how" in Islam. It is prohibited to question the words of Muhammad and his god in the Quran. It is also very costly to criticize Muslim leaders who are closely attached to Islam. As a result, you do not have freedom if you continue to be a Muslim.

But the God of the Bible calls all of us to be accountable to weigh before accepting a prophesy or instruction. I wouldn't follow Jesus if He did not authorize me to use the words "what, why and how" in order to understand whether His Path was the true Path or not. Freedom is the first step in following Jesus. That's why He even respects the freedom of His enemies also.

So, I am following a God who has created me with freedom of choice. My freedom is the most important thing for God. No one has a right to impose his belief on me. Isn't this amazing? I therefore asked Jesus to establish me on His root which guarantees my freedom in every aspect, both worldly and spiritually. On His root I am enabled and prepared to pursue just, kind, loving and peaceful relationships with people from every nation, language, race and color. There is not a single enemy for me among humanity in the entire world. My enemy is only Satan who is against the freedom of choice and wants to keep people in the darkness of indifference or ignorance.

Do you realize now how the true God or standard or foundation or root affects every part of your life and prepares you wholly to enjoy your life and become a light for all? This light in you will never allow any agent of darkness to build a nest in you in order to make a mess of your own life or your relationships with others.

I am following this God now. Jesus established me on such a root which has given me a new identity with a new heart, a new worldview with new political, social and moral values so that I can care for all, including my enemies. Jesus Christ revealed to me that a better choice necessitates a thorough understanding from the root of things to their branches. We are all in desperate need of making good choices if we wish to have a healthy life. I listened to Him in order to make a good choice. I followed the truthful root in Jesus, then every branch of my life became comforting and amazing. The first comfort I received was the spiritual confidence about my afterlife. I realized that if a person is established on the root of God, he will be on that root forever since the root is eternal. I am now certain that I belong to God one hundred per cent of my life on earth and I will also be with Him forever. I should not worry about hell since I am established on God's root. Isn't this confidence amazing and comforting? It is.

Before meeting Jesus Christ, like all Muslims, I worried about my future in Islam. I wished to overcome the lack of confidence which Islam had left in me about the afterlife. The Quran says that nobody knows about his future, and Muhammad also said continually that he was unsure about his future. This was troubling me. I was asked to do everything for the god of Islam, follow the footsteps of Muhammad, yet all for an unknown future. But by reading Christian literature I realized, "if God is compassionate, He should prove His very compassion to me in my life on earth. He does this by giving me confidence that I belong to Him now and will be with Him forever."

The highest compassion I expect to see from God is to save me from my ambiguity. My spiritual assurance is more important than all other things He has given to me. I need salvation now. I need to overcome spiritual uncertainty now to become free. The true and compassionate God never asks people to put their trust in Him for an unknown future. Actually, God's major mission is to release people from any ambiguity about their future and gain their trust.

It is the same in our daily life. We do not put our trust in someone unless he proves his trustworthiness. It is here that we see a great weakness in the Quran in comparison with the Gospel of Jesus Christ.

The Gospel teaches, if you follow Jesus Christ now you will be saved now and forever. But the Quran teaches, if you follow Muhammad, you are not saved now, and are not sure whether you'll be saved in the afterlife or not. So, by following Jesus I was able to experience the compassion of God in my life on earth, be saved and have assurance for eternity.

The second amazing thing I received from the root of Jesus Christ is that I am a child of light, love, kindness, justice, righteousness, holiness and peace. These are my identities and those of every person who follows Jesus. If God is the light, love, kind, just, righteous, holy and peace-loving God, I carry all these values with me since I am established on His foundation. I now have these tools and know how to deal with friends, opponents and enemies. I am and need to be a light to friends, opponents and enemies, be kind to them and avoid being unjust to anyone with any excuse. I need to stretch my heart to them lovingly and encourage them to search for the best way together for having a long-lasting relationship.

Isn't this amazing when you believe that even your worst enemies can become your best friends if you approach them with loving wisdom and plead with them to find the best way for building a long-lasting relationship? It is amazing. I myself have experienced such amazing things in my relationship with some of those who did not like me because of my faith in Christ. Let me give you a couple of examples.

One day a gentleman said to me that he did not like to hear anything from Christianity as it was rubbish to him. I asked him whether he truly believed it was rubbish. He said yes. I told him, "Then I need your help. I am carrying it in my heart. I honestly do not like to carry rubbish in my heart. Could you please help me to get rid of this rubbish?" "Where do you want me to help you?", he asked me. I said to him that Jesus says: "Love your neighbors as yourself, love your enemies and bless them, and love your spouse as your own body." He is telling us that the best tools for you to build a long-lasting friendship are love and kindness. "Which one of these look like a rubbish to you?" He said that they are good. I told him again that Jesus said: "The greatest of you must become the servant of all." Jesus is trying to say that only modest leadership can lead people in justice and peace. Dictatorship is unable to walk hand-in-hand with peace and justice. Where do you find rubbish in this? He said he never knew these things were in the Gospel. He apologized me and accepted to read the Gospel.

In another instance, an Imam of a mosque started to attack me since I was revealing some verses of the Quran to people. I told him, "Sir, don't you believe that your religion is the last and perfect religion? Why should the follower of a religion use violence if it is called perfect and thereby has perfect wisdom for a peaceful conversation with other? You call Christianity imperfect. If that is the case, then I need to use violence if my religion is called imperfect, but conversely you are using violence and I am peaceful."

His conscience was touched and he noticed that I was right in challenging him for a peaceful talk. My short and peaceful talks with him became a good introduction for our 6 months friendly conversation. He eventually gave his heart to Jesus. An imam of a mosque left Islam and became a follower of Jesus!

Isn't this amazing to you that I no longer respond to violence with violence? I have come from a violent background. I was a committed Muslim leader, politician and scholar. I had learned that violence was the only response to those who said "no" to Islam. But now under the leadership of Jesus Christ I approach my opponents with His love, kindness and logic, touch their consciences so that they can have an opportunity to think deep, find the truth and become my friends. My journey from Islam to Christ has become a chance of blessings to all, including my opponents.

This is my story. I am touched by Jesus Christ, renewed and have eternal confidence. I am a new person now, free to use my mind, my heart and my conscience in order to draw the attention of people to the real freedom. Thank you so much for listening to my story.

Reflection Time 3

1. Is it reasonable if I do not learn good things, but expect others to be good?
2. Why do we need to get our minds, hearts and consciences into action?
3. How much does our belief affect our spiritual and social life? If the effect is negative, should we search for an alternative?

4. If you believe in God, is it good to know Him, have a personal relationship with Him and receive eternal confidence?
5. Why did Daniel put his trust in Jesus?
6. In what way or ways you can identify with Daniel?

God – Does God Exist?

Philosophical discussions about the existence and non-existence of God have their roots deep in history. The historical evidences take us to the fifth century Before Christ (BC), before Socrates, to those who described the work of nature without God for the first time. The name of the prominent person of this era and movement was Thales.

The philosophy of disbelief in God became very vocal after the Communist and Darwinian movements. Later, this even took a strong political stand against the spread of God and Creation philosophies.

Those who do not believe in the existence of God say: A God does not exist if he cannot be seen or touched. We are not sure whether God exists or not since science has not proven the existence of God yet. They therefore guess that the world came into being randomly and by accident and cannot have a Creator. But those who believe in the existence of God say: Since everything that exists has an inventor and creator, the existence of the world is also an indication to its own Creator.

Evidences against the random philosophy of existence

The first evidence is the make-up of everything

Everything in the world has an orderly and well-formed structure which cannot be by accident. Anytime we see a regular order in something it means that there has been intellect, knowledge and management behind the establishment of that regularity. If this is the case, then the random philosophy of existence not only does not make sense, but will also be against the rationality of science.

A second evidence is the way that members of the body function

Every member of a human or animal body is positioned in its place with an extraordinary intelligence for a particular task and purpose. This intelligence does not go hand-in-hand with the theory of random philosophy. For example, a giraffe has a 13kg (29lb) heart with two times more pressure than the pressure of an elephant's heart, in order to run the blood through a longer neck to its head. It has a very specific vessel[2] near the brain which functions like a sponge and absorbs blood gently when the head is down in order to reduce the pressure of the blood, otherwise the head would explode. If the pressure is too high, the sponge signals the giraffe to lift its head before damage happens.

Is it possible to describe this amazing intelligent design via random philosophy? Absolutely not.

A third evidence is the moral practices among humanity

Moral practices in daily life cannot be the result of random incidents. For example, without an experience and a standard we will not be able to say, this one is good but that one is bad, or this wrong but the other right. But, if we rely on our experiences or standards like this, then the random philosophy will be meaningless. Why? Because we have experienced them in the past, and the knowledge of the past experiences is now our life standard. With this information we can

---

[2] https://en.wikipedia.org/wiki/Giraffe#Neck; http://www.africam.com/wildlife/giraffe_drinking.

march ahead towards the future with open eyes in order to avoid negative and harmful things.

So, we can see that standards are the result of our evaluating ability and intelligent decision-making rather than accidentally, in order to lead us towards our desired goals. Therefore, random philosophy is just a theory and does not match the practical aspects of our life.

The moral order of every family in the world is also against random philosophy

Throughout history parents, even those who do not believe in God, avoided marrying their children. Relying on such a premade order is sharply against random philosophy. In addition, no one can say in a random incident that this person is my chosen spouse or that is the child we decided to have; because selecting or arranging do not match a random life or philosophy.

So you see that everything in the world, including science, is not compatible with the random philosophy of existence but points to the existence of a Creator who designed and created the universe.

The world is created by God. We just need to look at the things around us closely in order to understand this.

Who is this God?

Well, God is defined differently by many religions. But which one is telling the truth? It is not my plan in this book to discuss various religions' approaches to God, but I am aiming to compare the Muslims' and Christians' views of God. Do Islam and Christianity view God differently? Let us see as much as we can.

God in Islam and Christianity

Can God have a relationship with people in either of these beliefs?

The Bible says: God is the revealing God by nature. He builds personal relationships as He had personal relationships with many people in the Bible.[3]

---

[3] The God of the Bible is personal and relational, He therefore cannot be an absolutely invisible God, but the visible One. He is visible by his nature, as He revealed Himself to some in the OT, spoke directly to

The Quran says: Allah is non-revealing by nature and cannot have a personal relationship with people. This is similar to Greek philosophy: In Greek Philosophy God does not have personality and cannot reveal himself. The reason Muslim scholars borrowed from Greek philosophy is because Allah's characteristic could only match Greek philosophy.

We read in the Bible that God sees, hears, speaks directly to people and shows Himself to anyone He chooses. But the Quran says in Sura Al An'am (6) verse 103 that Allah sees but is invisible, and Sura Ash-shura (42) verse 51 says that Allah speaks to no one but behind a veil. So, the Quran says that God hides and never reveals Himself, but the Bible says that God reveals Himself.

Now before entering a logical discussion, let me ask you a simple question. Would you love to see your Creator face-to-face?

I have been amazed so many times by the responses of many people from various religious

---

all prophets and revealed Himself in the NT as a Man. He hides Himself in some circumstances depending on His own ethics or decision.

backgrounds who said that they would love to see their Creator. Contrary to Islamic view, some great Middle Eastern Muslim philosophers, theologians and poets also desired to see God face to face.

In brief, I want to tell you that God never desires to hide Himself from you if you desire to see Him.

Why God shouldn't hide Himself

God shows His love personally

God is the God of love; He does not hide His love. You never call a person lovely unless that person reveals his or her love in relationships. God is the same; He reveals His love in relationships with you and with His creatures. As a result, God must build a relationship with us first and then reveal His love to us. God planned for Creation in the beginning and included His love in that plan too. In Creation, He revealed Himself to Adam and Eve, and they were able to see God and His love personally.

If your god does not reveal himself, he therefore is not a relational god and does not have any interest in your life.

We will be able to know God better if He reveals Himself

Each individual who is personally created by God needs to know his creator personally. Isn't it better to know God personally without mediation? Knowing a person without a mediator creates intimacy. Suppose you want to build a family, won't it be more beneficial for you to know your future life partner personally and unite with her or him? With God it is the same. If you want to unite with God, you need to know him personally.

God's words won't relate to us directly if we do not know Him personally. On the other hand, no one can make God better known to us than God Himself. Why then shouldn't God make Himself known to us personally? God doesn't hide himself. If your religion says that God does not reveal himself and does not make himself known, that religion cannot be Godly.

If a person does not know God personally, can he be a messenger of God? No. A true messenger of God is sent by God Himself. If a person has not seen God, hasn't heard His voice and does not know Him, with what logic can he say that he is from God? There is no logic in that. A genuine messenger should have a direct relationship with the person of God, with His voice and words, otherwise he will not be genuine in his claim that he is from God. And, if there is no basis for reason in a religion, then deception, force or sword will be the means of making a message acceptable. Therefore, if your religion teaches that your prophet hasn't met God personally, then you need to search for another belief which promotes personal relationships between God and His messengers.

God of love desires to lead people personally

Haven't you heard people say, "May God lead you"? This is because people desire to be led by God personally. I am sure that you all agree with me that God is the best when it comes to justice, righteousness, holiness and kindness. Who else then can lead people better than God? No one. God knows if He Himself leads you personally, then Satan will not be able to get close to you. But if a prophet leads you, you will not be immune from Satan's influence. For this reason, God does not hide Himself, but loves to reveal Himself to lead you personally. Therefore, if you allow God to lead you personally, it will be safer for you instead of being led by a middle-man or a prophet. As a result, if your religion does not give you a chance to have a personal relationship with God, and obligates you to blindly follow your prophet, that religion cannot be from God.

God desires to establish justice on earth personally

If God is the ultimate authority in justice and Satan the ultimate authority in injustice, who else other than God can triumph over Satan and establish the justice in your life on earth? No one except God. If this is the case, then God needs to reveal Himself and establish justice on earth. Because a prophet cannot overcome Satan personally. Thus, if your religion teaches that God does not reveal Himself personally to fight Satan for us, it is misleading you and is unaware of the way God's justice is established.

God desires to save humankind personally

Satan is the highest authority in injustice and has chained humans. If this is the case, who can then save this chained humanity from Satan and sin? Can a chained person save himself from Satan? No. First of all, he is in a spiritual prison and a prisoner cannot save himself. Secondly, Satan is the head of this spiritual prison, mightier than any human, hates humanity, and also does not believe in the freedom or salvation of any human. No man can save himself. Every human being needs God to come and save him or her personally. For God to come means that He does not hide Himself.

Your religion is misleading you if it says that you can save yourself from Satan with your good deeds. If we are not spiritually saved and free, this ungodly situation keeps us from being able to perform any heavenly deed that can satisfy God. God is the source of love and justice. You will not be able to think, speak and act for God truly unless you reside in God's love and justice first. In other words, your deeds cannot be relevant to God unless you are united with God and your relationship with sin and Satan is cancelled. God's desire is for humanity to be free from Satan first. Freedom from Satan is the beginning of good deeds for God. In other words, God's first mission is to reveal Himself to free you. The deeds that really satisfy God start after you are saved and free.

So the God of love does not hide Himself and does not delay salvation for the afterlife

Is it fair to leave the salvation of a person for tomorrow while he is crying for it today?

If Satan has separated humanity from God and His kingdom on earth and made them sinners, their salvation also must happen on earth. Don't those who are forced to live apart from one another in this world desire to unite as soon as possible with each other? Won't it be more painful if their unity is delayed? Both God's and our hearts are the same. God does not want to delay the visit. He reveals Himself to us here on earth. Our hearts also will not get rest if our salvation is delayed. Therefore, your religion cannot be in harmony with the heart of God if it hides God and leaves salvation for the afterlife.

You see how the Bible reveals God, but the Quran hides Him. It is not pleasant when someone hides the most beautiful person from you. Jesus taught that God never hides Himself from you. He loves you. Also, Jesus is the architect of these realistic and logical words which I shared with you. If these words seem right to your heart, you also need to follow Jesus.

Reflection Time 4

1. Why is it unreasonable to believe that the world exists by accident or by itself?

2. Most people in the world want to have a good plan for their future. A plan requires a standard. A good standard cannot be established without comparing past experiences. Can the random theory of existence be compatible with such willful management and decision-making in our lives?

3. Do we have the capacity to reason[4] and discover the truth?

---

[4] There are people among the followers of all religions who say that their God is the only true God and their God has given the best or perfect religion to them. Imagine, if all religions' followers in the world have the same mindset, do not believe in comparison, reasoning and searching for the Truth with others or live without any challenges or questions. How would it be possible to discover the true God if there is no comparison?

4. Look at Romans 2:14-16, then II Corinthians 4:2 and finally Galatians 3:24 and then see if we are able to help people to become aware of the law (witness) of God in themselves through their consciences and to allow the law of God to take them to Jesus.

5. Deep in their hearts, do people desire to see and unite with their Creator?

6. Why shouldn't the true God hide himself?

7. If a person does not know God personally, can he be a messenger of God?

8. Why leave the question of salvation for the afterlife if it is available today? Isn't it good to be saved now?

How to Differentiate Between the True God and False God?

There is only one God in the universe, but the gods other religions have been introducing are much different from this God. Which religion is introducing the true God?

Can we know which religion has the true God?

Yes. We have eyes to read and see, ears to hear and listen, brains to compare, hearts to evaluate and discover the truth and a conscience to stand for the truth no matter the cost. So we have the capacity to search for the true God, find Him and live with Him. Anyone can read or hear about the characteristics of gods in different religions' books. We can compare them with each other and then we are able to distinguish the true God from false gods.

What are the criteria for discovering the true God?

There are:

1. Philosophical Criteria

2. Doctrinal Criteria
3. Social, political, economic and moral criteria

Philosophical criteria

The first philosophical criterion is that God must be personal

God must be personal in order to be able to build personal relationships with people and help them. An impersonal god cannot build any personal relationship with a person, save him or guide him. Such a god is therefore helpless and hopeless. For example, god in Islam is impersonal. Since Muhammad, the prophet of Islam, was unable to see God, he pronounced God as absolutely invisible and a non-revealing god. After his death, Muslim philosophers based their philosophy on Muhammad's experience and defined God as impersonal, inaccessible and unknowable.

If a god is absolutely invisible, he cannot then reveal his thoughts, words or acts. This also means that he has no thought to reveal his plan, no word to speak about his plan and no working ability to put his plan into action. In other words, he cannot speak because only a person speaks, not a non-person. He also cannot create, because creation needs words; as we say, "God said and it became". Since the god in Islam cannot speak, the creation cannot be attributed to him.

So the impersonal nature of the god in Islam did not allow him to reveal himself to Muhammad or to have a personal relationship with him. Since he cannot have a personal relationship with anyone, he will be unable to help and save. Because helping or saving requires revelation and personal relationship.

Many Muslims are praying every day and asking their god to put them on the right path. How can he put people on the right path since he is not able to reveal himself to guide and protect them? Guidance and protection can only be defined if there is a personal relationship, whereas the Quran says that Allah does not reveal himself and does not relate to anyone personally. So, the first and fundamental criterion for the true God is that he must reveal himself to save people from Satan and sin. As a result, if the god or ultimate reality in your religion does not reveal himself , then he is not the true God.

The second philosophical criterion is that God's presence must be everywhere and functional

God is able to be with us in a practical way. Since both God and us have personal characteristics, we are also able to sense God's presence personally if He is with and in us.

We have to have legitimate reasons if we proclaim God's presence within us. Many Muslims dismiss the philosophy of the Quran about God and proclaim that God is with them. I have heard so many times that Muslims claim "God is in their blood. He is closer to them than their jugular vein." Is God really with Muslims? Can this claim be proven by reason? No. Let me describe why not?

If God is with you, this means that God is with you with all his assurance, kindness and love. Since He is the good, kind, merciful and compassionate God, He, therefore, never desires to leave you uncertain about any part of your life, but gives you 100% confidence about your future. If you say that he does not give you confidence or in other words he does not guide you perfectly, then he is not the true God.

You, as a Muslim, are saying that God is with you, the light for your path and guides you perfectly. Let me ask you another very significant spiritual question. Are you saved and certain that you will go to heaven or paradise? Your response, your prophet's response and the Quran's response are all "No". This means that your god hasn't given you any confidence about your future. How can the God of assurance be with you, but you are still unsure? This means that the God of assurance or the true God is not with you, otherwise, you would have assurance. In other words, your religion is unable to take you to the true God. So the presence of God can be proved in us only when we are saved by God here on earth and have the confidence of going to heaven or paradise.

The third philosophical criterion is that God must be knowable

The true God is the kind of God who you will be able to know personally and the One you can follow based on your own personal experience with Him. You do not follow a person whom you do not know. God is the same. He doesn't want you to follow him blindly or through a middle person. He wants you to be with Him through your own personal experience with Him.

Doctrinal criteria for discovering the true God

The first doctrinal criterion is that God must be absolutely righteous

This means that an absolutely righteous God cannot have bad and immoral deeds or make them legitimate; because, His nature is perfectly good and far from evil. Therefore, if you see in the book of your god that he is the creator of sin and evil or has legitimized them in some circumstances, that god cannot be the true God. You need to evaluate the words and deeds of your god, if you want to know whether your belief is heavenly or not.

The second doctrinal criterion is that God must be absolutely a just God

This means that God cannot say or do unjust things. For example: God cannot give his prophet or the leaders more rights than others, because He is absolutely just. He cannot give men more rights than women or ask men to beat their wives. He cannot give some of his followers more rights than others. He cannot promote sectarianism and encourage people to ignore the rights of others. If you see your god has legitimized such unjust things, he cannot be the true and just God.

The third doctrinal criterion is that God must be absolutely a holy God

This means that God cannot sin, create or inspire sin, or legitimize sin under any circumstances. Can a holy God corrupt others and make them sinners? Not at all. Therefore, if you see that your god has corrupted others, made them sinners, he cannot be holy. Such a god cannot be a good role model for people.

The fourth doctrinal criterion is that God must be a loving and kind God

This means that God respects and loves people, and draws their attention to Himself through wisdom, kindness and peaceful means. Since He Himself desired to create us, He Himself must also provide the kindest and loveliest means of unity for people. Like a parent to his children, He must approach you with the loveliest and most educational manner so that you can run to Him with zeal and unite with Him. God should not be like a cruel person who ignores your freedom of choice and deals with you unjustly. If your god does not have such a love and kindness, he is not the true God, and his religion also cannot create love, kindness and peace among people.

Now is the time for me to give you some social, political, economic and moral criteria for discovering the true God

Social criteria

The true God is absolutely far from every kind of discrimination concerning gender, race, nationality, belief, position or any other thing that could separate people. Your god cannot be the true God if he gives more rights to men than women, to masters than slaves, to his followers than others.

Political criteria

The true God establishes and promotes a modest kind of leadership instead of dictatorship. In the eyes of the true God, the greatest among people is the most humble among all and a servant to all. Your god cannot be the true God, if he gives a dictatorial role to his prophet or to any of his followers.

Economic criteria

The true God believes that people, both followers and others, deserve to receive equal compensation for the same time and work. The true God does not limit the rights, ignore nor issue heavy taxes on non-followers.

Moral criteria

The true God never legitimizes lying, deceiving or any kind of immorality no matter what the circumstances may be. The true God is a holy God, and his holiness is always against sin whether it is committed by a follower or a non-follower. Your god cannot be the true God if he allows or encourages his followers to deceive others or lie to them.

There are many false gods and beliefs in the world. You won't be able to understand whether you are following the true God or a false god unless you learn who the true God is. These criteria helped me to find the true God and to have amazing experiences with my Creator and Savior. My prayer is that they become useful in your life too so that you can reside in the eternal joy of God.

Reflection Time 5

1. If we are created in God's image, would we not be capable of knowing our Creator?
2. If we are able to distinguish between right and wrong, good and evil, should we not also be able to differentiate the true God from the false one?
3. If a god inspires sins, can he be the true God?
4. Is it good to have a personal relationship with God or not?
5. When are we able to prove that we have the presence of God within us?
6. Who can introduce God better; the one who is in relationship with God or one who does not have any personal experience with God?
7. If you believe that God is personal, pray to Him to be your personal guide.

The Difference between the God of Islam and the God of Christianity

Some people say that Muslims and Christians are all following the same God. They do not know that the texts in Islam are introducing a different god than in Christianity. For this reason, I want to compare the words of the Quran with the Bible so that you can see the great difference between the god of Islam and the God of Christianity.

The first difference: The god of Islam is unable to help people

As I discussed in my previous talk, the god of Islam is believed to be non-relational by the Quran and Muslim scholars. He therefore cannot build relationships in order to help. You may say that though the god of Islam does not build relationships personally, he sends his angel to relate and help. This is a wrong philosophy. Why? Because, if the angel is relational, then he cannot have a relationship with the non-relational god and be his messenger to humanity. An impersonal god cannot have any personal messenger.

So you can see that the god in Islam cannot be expected to help because of his nature. But the God of Christianity is able to help. The God of the Bible is a personal, relational, functional God and can help people. In the book of Isaiah chapter 45 verse 2, the Christians' God says: I will go before you and will level the mountains. (NIV) So you see that God is walking with His people.

God has created humanity for a purpose. To give purpose to our lives, God's continuous personal presence and guidance are necessary. The words such as "presence and guidance" can only be used for a relational God not for non-relational gods. That's why the apostles of Jesus Christ wrote that they witnessed the revelation of God. The Apostle John says that God became flesh, lived among us, and we saw his glory …. full of grace and truth (read John 1:14).

So you see that the god of Islam is unable to reveal himself to help. But the God of Christianity is the revealing God by nature, reveals Himself in order to help, save and guide people personally.

The second difference: The god of Islam is the creator of good and bad

The God of Christianity is only the Creator of good things. The god of Islam is called mighty in creating both good and evil and for inspiring sin in humankind and corrupting them. The God of Christianity is called mighty only for good deeds. His nature is totally holy and righteous. He cannot even think about corrupting people or creating sin.

Sura Al Hadid (57) verse 22, Sura Al A'raf (7) verse 16 and Sura Ash Shams (91) verse 8 all in the Quran confirm that the god of Islam designed all misfortune, sin and corruption from eternity and brought them into existence in creation. But the God of the Bible is far from designing, planning or creating sin and corruption. The loving, righteous, just, peace-loving and kind God cannot corrupt people. His job is to purify them. If the god of Islam is the creator of untruth and sin, he will not be genuinely able to call people to truth or guide them in truth.

By attributing untruth and sin to God, the Quran is misleading people. The creation of sin is sin in itself so the god of Islam is therefore a sinner, whereas the true God cannot be a sinner. Secondly, people will see no reason for avoiding sin since the god of Islam was unable to avoid it. If a god has created sin for people, why shouldn't people open their hearts to sin? A sin-creating god is an obstacle to the spread of truth in a society. In reality, the truthful God cannot create untruth and sin because of His holy nature. Therefore, the god that the Quran is portraying is not the true God.

The God of the Bible Is the Truthful God. The Gospel of Jesus Christ says in 1 John chapter 2 verse 21 that "No lie is of the truth." (KJV) And it says in James chapter 3 verse 17, "The wisdom that is from above is first truly pure, then peaceable, gentle, easy to be entreated, full of mercy and good fruits, without partiality and without hypocrisy." (MKJV)

The third difference: The god of Islam is against freedom of choice

Sura Al Ahzab (33) in verse 36 says that nobody has the right to challenge the words of Muhammad, the prophet of Islam. But the Christians' God says in the book of Deuteronomy chapter 18 verse 22 that you should not accept the words of prophets blindly; instead, you have the right to reject or accept them with knowledge.

The fourth difference: The god of Islam is against equal opportunity

We understand from the Quran and Islamic traditional books that Muhammad has more rights than other Muslims, Muslim men than Muslim women, light-skinned Muslims than black Muslims, and Muslims in general than non-Muslims.[5] But faith in Christ Jesus is what makes each of you equal with each other, whether you are a Jew or a non-Jew, a slave or a free person, a man or a woman. (Galatians 3:28; Colossians 3:11)

The fifth difference: The god of Islam believes in superiority of men

Sura An Nisa (4) verse 34 and Sura Sad (38) verse 44 in the Quran say that men have the right to beat their wives. In Sura An Nisa (4) verses 15 to 16, men even have the right to lock their wives in a room for immorality until they die. But for the

---

[5] See the following references and the references under the title "Leadership in Islam Is Chaotic".

same immorality, men get some slashes only and walk free.

The Gospel of Jesus Christ never allows such heartbreaking things; it says in Ephesians chapter 5 verses 25 and 28 that a man must love his wife as his own body.

The sixth difference: The god of Islam cherishes discrimination

The Quran in Sura Al Tawba (9) verse 28 says that non-Muslims are unclean; in Sura Al Anfal (8) verse 55 it says that non-Muslims are the worst of beasts; in Sura Al Bagharah (2) verse 65; Sura Al Maeda (5) verse 60 and Sura Al Juma (62) verse 5 it says that Jews and Christians are pigs, monkeys and donkeys. But the Gospel of Jesus Christ says that there is no difference between Jews and others, all are the same in the eyes of God who created all with the same image and hand.

The seventh difference: The god of Islam is the cause of immorality

Sura Al Anfal (8) verse 30 and Sura Yunus (10) verse 21 say that Allah is the best of deceivers.

Sura Al Bagharah (2) verse 225, Sura Al-e Imran (3) verse 28 and Sura An Nahl (16) verse 106 encourage Muslims to lie if conditions necessitate. But the Gospel in 1 John chapter 2 verse 21 says: No lie comes from the truth. (NIV) The Torah says in Exodus chapter 23 verses 1 and 2: Do not give a false report, do not become a false witness for a criminal. Stand for justice no matter how dishonest the majority may be. (NIV)

Do you see the difference? Christians' God says you should not lie, but the god of Islam says, well it depends.

The eighth difference: The god of Islam produces dictators

Sura Al Anbiya (21) verse 23 says: Allah cannot be questioned as to what he does, but people are questioned for their actions. Sura Al Ahzab (33) verse 36 says: Nobody can have any choice when it comes to Allah's and Muhammad's decision. Sura Al Mujadila (58) verses 20 and 21 say: Those who resist Allah and His Apostle will be among those most humiliated. Allah has decreed: "It is I and My apostles who must prevail": For Allah is One full of strength, able to enforce His Will.

You see that the leadership in Islam is based on dictatorship from the root to the branches. But let us see how the leadership in the Bible is designed for people's freedom.

The Torah in Deuteronomy chapter 18 verse 22 says if a prophet is not right, do not be afraid of him, and do not obey him.

> When a prophet speaks in the name of the LORD, if the word does not come to pass or come true, that is a word that the LORD has not spoken; the prophet has spoken it presumptuously. You need not be afraid of him. (Deuteronomy 18:22, ESV)

In Isaiah chapter 1 verse 18, even God says to people: Come and reason together. You see that in the Bible people have the right to use their God-given freedom of choice in questioning even the statements of God or His prophets and stay away from blind obedience. Why? Because the freedom of choice is from God and He respects that freedom. It becomes more amazing when the leadership comes to Jesus. As the leader, He washed the feet of His own disciples. (John 13: 5) And about the quality of a leader He says: You know that the rulers of the nations exercise dominion over them, and they who are great exercise authority over them. However, it shall not be so among you. But whoever desires to be great among you, let him be your servant. And whoever desires to be chief among you, let him be your servant. (Matthew 20:25-27, MKJV)

So you see that Jesus is teaching that you need to destroy the seed of dictatorship in your own heart. This will enable you to respect the freedom of each individual no matter what their nationality, race, color or belief is.

The ninth difference: The god of Islam lacks wisdom

What kind of wisdom is this that Allah himself places people in sin and lawlessness, then asks them to praise him for what he has done? True wisdom does not chain people in sin, but becomes a light of freedom for them. The God of the Bible did not create people with sin. Humans were themselves the cause of their own fall into sin. But God with a fatherly heart took and is still taking sacrificial initiatives to save them. There is a huge difference between the god of Islam and the God of Christians.

The tenth difference: The god of Islam himself corrupted Satan and made him an enemy to humanity

Sura Al A'raf (7) in verse 16 says that Satan was corrupted and made the deceiver by Allah. Why? Because, he loved to create a problem maker for people, especially for those who would oppose him. Isn't it strange, this god is then called compassionate in every chapter of the Quran?

The God of Christians is so different. He did not corrupt Satan. Satan himself misused his freedom of choice, rebelled against God and became the cause of sin and lawlessness in the world. (Genesis 1:31; Ezekiel 28:14-17; Jude 6) God is against Satan in every aspect and desires to release people, even his enemies, from the hand of Satan.

The eleventh difference: The god of Islam uses demons to spread Islam

Sura Al Jinn (72) in verses 1-13 says that Allah uses demons to spread Islam. The book of Muhammad's life-story (by Ibn Ishaq) says in pages 106 and 107 that he was not sure whether the very first revealed chapter, Sura Al Alagh (96), of the Quran was inspired in him by Satan or Allah.

The reason that the god of Islam uses demons in his mission is because he carries the attributes of a pagan god. Only in paganism are demons trusted. The true God cannot walk hand-in-hand with demons for the spread of his religion. So you see that Islamic culture is hard to separate from pagan culture. Pagan culture and beliefs have become part of the Quran, a book that is called holy and heavenly. In the Quran we read that demons are even servants to prophets.

The God of Christians not only does not use demons in spreading His words, but frees people from demons and heals them. God is holy, just and righteous, and knows that demons spread injustice and they never speak the message of truth.

The twelfth difference: The god of Islam leaves his righteous followers uncertain about their future

The Quran in Sura Mariam (19) verse 68 says that righteous Muslims are taken to hell immediately after they die and they will wait there with the evil ones for the judgment day. This has created great fear among committed Muslims, including Muhammad, and they are unsure whether they will be able to pass the judgment. This spiritual fear of uncertainty has torn the hearts of committed Muslims and none of them has a sure response to the question if they'll be saved or not. The response is, "Only Allah knows."

But the righteous Christians will go to God in heaven immediately after they die. The question of life or death for Christians is solved in this life. You enter the kingdom of eternal life during your lifetime on earth if you choose to follow Jesus who is alive and in heaven. If you do, you will pass the judgment and never be judged in the afterlife. You will directly be taken to heaven.

The thirteenth difference: The god of Islam is not accessible in this world

In Islam, there is no access to God's kingdom in this world. Since God is not accessible, his kingdom also is not accessible.

In daily life, Muslims normally say that God is with them. But this is against the doctrine of the Quran and Islam which believe that God does not reveal Himself. However, the God of Christians is the revealing and accessible God. He has revealed Himself in Jesus Christ to save and unite you with Himself so that you can have eternal relationship with Him. After you allow Him to save you in the Name of Jesus, you will belong to Him forever, and nothing will be able to separate you from Him.

The fourteenth difference: The god of Islam has a heathenish heaven

There is no news of God's presence in Islam's paradise throughout the Quran. But the Quran continually promises Jihadists and those who gain Allah's favor will be in paradise, spending their time with lustrous maidens. (Quran 37:48; 78: 33) This was the pagan belief in Muhammad's time.

Unlike the Islamic paradise, the heaven in Christians' Holy Book is not a place for men's lust. It is the throne of God, a place of eternal joy and peace with God. In His Gospel Christ teaches us that His followers will be with God in heaven (John 14:1-6). The Gospel of Jesus Christ says:

A great multitude from every nation, from all tribes and peoples and languages will stand before the throne of God and praise Him for saving them. (Revelation 7: 9)

So you see that the heaven in Christians' Holy Book is absolutely far from the immoralities of Islamic paradise. The God of Christians is very different from the god of Islam. He is trustworthy and superior to Allah in every aspect (Revelation 19:16)

I gave you all these reasons so that you may become encouraged to read the Gospel of Jesus Christ yourself and see the truth with your own eyes. Thank you so much for spending time with me.

Reflection Time 6

1. Can the god of Islam walk with his people and give purpose to their lives? Why?
2. Why do all need to follow the God of the Bible, not the god of the Quran?
3. Do the attributes of the god of Islam affect people's lives if they follow him?
4. How important is it for us to follow the true God and reveal Him to others also?

5. Let us ask the true God to personally guide us so that we can become the reflection of His truth to others.

Can the God of Islam Be a God Guide?

We will not be able to respond to this question appropriately unless we understand the qualities of a good guide and the way he acts through the eyes of our consciences. Let us look at the qualities and actions of a good guide.

A good guide introduces a good and safe destination to his followers

You need to get to a certain place; he knows the way and you need his accurate, straight, sound and tender guidance. When a good guide promises to take you to the destination, it means that he is ready to stand behind his promise and put it into practice no matter what the cost may be. He guarantees you that you'll get there; especially because he is mighty to overcome every obstacle, then your confidence is 100%. A good guide knows the threats and dangers all the way to the destination and has the best solution to combat each one of them. A good guide never cooperates with evil planners to be a threat to his own followers but stands against them in order to create an unshakable trust in the hearts of his followers.

Does Allah have a safe and good destination for his followers and does he assure them that he himself will not be a threat to them? Does he have qualities that people can trust him to guide them safely? Let us see where the journey with Allah ends up

From the Quran in Sura Mariam (19) verses 67 to 72 we learn that Allah will take his righteous followers along with the evil ones and gather them inside Hell for judgment. After the judgment, the evil ones will remain in hell, but among the righteous ones some may be able to go to paradise if their good deeds outweigh their bad deeds and if they can cross the tiny bridge of Sirat[6].

---

[6] 'Sirat' is the narrowest bridge, as narrow and sharp as the edge of a knife, between hell and paradise in Islam. It is believed that only a righteous can cross it and enter paradise. However, even the prophet of Islam did not have confidence for being able to cross the bridge.

In these verses, the god of Islam is saying to his righteous Muslims, "Hey, you have been faithful to me more than others in order to make me happy. But I can't guarantee to reward you for it. You may still stay in hell and suffer for eternity." What a good guide!

You see that under the guidance of the god of Islam, evil ones are receiving what they deserve. They have done everything in this world they wanted, they knew that they deserved hell, and now Allah takes them to hell. But the poor righteous followers of Allah trusted Allah and deprived themselves of many things of the world, hoping that Allah would take them to paradise, but now they have the same destiny as evil ones. Wow!

So the message of the Quran is clear about unrighteous people; it does not have good news for them, they will remain in hell. But it also does not have good news for the righteous Muslims; they may stay in hell too. There is no doubt that Allah is the enemy of those who do not follow Islam. According to these verses, he does not seem to be friendly to his own righteous Muslims either. He acts as a mighty enemy against his righteous Muslims. He calls himself the "God of

Mercy" at the beginning of every Sura in the Quran but inflicts pain on his own righteous Muslims by taking them to hell on their way to judgment.

Why would a god, if he is merciful, treat the righteous in the same manner as unrighteous? Is this the Quranic definition of "Mercy"? If the mercy of Allah does not protect a righteous Muslim from the horrors of hell, what else may be concluded but that Allah's mercy is deceiving and tyrannical? This is a clear example of the misleading nature of Allah's leadership.

Shouldn't the true God take his righteous ones to heaven directly? Yes. The true God does. The God of the Bible does. But the god of Islam does not do that, because he is not the true God. No matter how righteous a Muslim may be for the god of Islam, he will take them first to hell, to that horrifying place, for judgment. And it is possible that they may stay there forever.

The Quran says that the entry to paradise is uncertain

Sura Luqman (31) in verse 34 says: The knowledge of the Hour is with Allah .... No soul can know what it will earn tomorrow ....

In other words, the god of Islam knows which righteous will remain in hell, but he never reveals that secret to anyone, even to Muhammad. He left all his righteous ones in uncertainty.

Aren't you shocked by the guidance of the god of Islam? He asks you to follow him, but you do not know where he is leading you. Do you follow someone who keeps his goal a secret and does not tell you where he is going to take you? If not, then how can you follow a god with the same characteristics? The god of Islam even leaves Muhammad in uncertainty

In Sura Al Ahghaf (46) verse 9 Muhammad says: I do not know what will be done with me or with you.

You see that even the prophet of Islam follows a god whose goal is unknown and for this reason he does not have any confidence of his salvation.

Isn't this sad that neither Muhammad nor any righteous Muslim knew or had confidence where they were heading to, but they pushed others to follow them to an unknown future too? They slaughtered many for not following them.

Even more sad is that Muhammad calls this uncertainty of Allah's guidance as "glad tiding"! In Sura Al A'raf (7) in verse 188 Muhammad says: If I had knowledge of the unseen, I should have multiplied all good, and no evil should have touched me: I am but a warner, and a bringer of glad tidings to those who have faith.

In this verse, Muhammad wants to say that instead of collecting the righteousness of God, he collected the evil works which are from Satan, because Allah did not give him enough knowledge and wisdom. At the end of this verse it says that Muhammad is a warner and giver of good news. He is calling the lack of knowledge, lack of good deeds and the touch of evil all together as "glad tiding" or good news. Can you believe this? Do you call the lack of knowledge a glad tiding? Do you call it "good news" if it is received from evil? Do you call the entry to hell good news? Do you call the uncertainty about paradise good news? Do you call the failure of righteous Muslims by

Allah good news? Do you really call Allah a good spiritual guide who caused his prophet and followers to remain uncertain about their future?

I wish you could find the time to read the Gospel and see how God looks after His followers. He teaches that nothing is more important than having assurance in life.

Future of Muhammad vs. the future of the prophets in the Bible

Let us see the difference between the future of Muhammad and the future of the prophets of the Bible.

Exodus chapter 32 verses 31-32 in the book of Torah it says that the name of Moses is written in the eternal book and he belongs to heaven. So, when Moses was living among his followers, he was aware that he was saved and God had prepared a place in heaven for him. The prophet Daniel says in his book chapter 12 verse 1 that the names of the followers of God are in the eternal book of life. This prophet of the Bible is saying that no fear should overcome the followers of the true God, because their eternal place is with God in heaven.

The names of Moses, Daniel, other prophets and all of God's followers are in the book of life. But the Quran says that neither Muhammad's nor any other Muslim's names are in the book of life. No one is certain of his future in Islam. Do you see the difference?

Jesus Christ guides His followers and gives them assurance

The Gospel teaches that from the time you place your faith in Jesus your relationship with hell is cancelled, you are protected from evil. Assurance of salvation is the central message of the Gospel for life on earth, because the true God does not leave people in uncertainty.

Jesus said in the Gospel of John chapter 5 verse 24: Truly, truly, I say to you, He who hears My Word and believes on Him who sent Me has everlasting life and shall not come into condemnation, but has passed from death to life. (MKJV)

Isn't it sad that Muslim leaders call the Torah and Gospel of assurance the imperfect books, but call the Quran the perfect book although it lacks assurance?

Let me give you more shocking things about the guiding attributes of Allah. Not only is Allah not a good guide, he is also misleading according to the Quran Sura Ibrahim (14) in verse 4 says that Allah leads astray whomever he wills.

Imagine a sign hanging over the chest of a guide which says, "I lead astray". Do you put your trust in that person to guide you? If not, then neither should you trust Allah who leads astray.

Let me give you a more heart-breaking example of Allah's guidance. Sura An Nisa (4) in verse 88 says: Oh Muhammad, for him whom Allah leads astray, you shall by no means find a pathway.

The god of Islam is saying in this chapter of the Quran that he leads you astray in a way that even the mediation of Muhammad becomes worthless. Why do you want to follow someone who leads you astray in a way that there will be no solution for your return? So you can see that you are face to face with a god in Islam who clearly says to you that he himself is a threat to your spiritual life and no one can save you if you trust him.

For this reason, I left Islam. I realized that the god of Islam not only was not a good guide, but was a threat to my spiritual life too. So, to stay a Muslim was nothing but a spiritual loss for me.

Now, let me give you some more examples from the Bible. You will be amazed at the loving heart of the God of the Bible for His followers, and understand my reason for following the Christians' God. See what the God of the Bible does for His followers.

Jacob says in Torah (Genesis 48:15): God has been my shepherd all my life long to this day. (ESV)

The prophet David says in Psalm chapter 23 verses 1 and 3: The LORD is my shepherd; ... He restores my soul. He leads me in paths of righteousness for his name's sake. (ESV)

The prophet Isaiah says: God will tend his flock like a shepherd; he will gather the lambs in his arms; he will carry them in his bosom, and gently lead those that are with young. (Isaiah 40:11, MKJV)

The prophet Ezekiel says: I myself will be the shepherd of my sheep, and I myself will make them lie down, declares the Lord GOD. (Ezekiel 34:15, ESV)

See what Jesus says: I am the good shepherd. The good shepherd lays down his life for the sheep. (John 10: 11, ESV)

The heart of God in the Bible is so different to the heart of god in the Quran.

Let me give you some more examples of how the god of Islam cannot be true and a good guide.

In the beginning the god of Islam believed that there should not be compulsion in religion.

When Muhammad was in Mecca and he did not have many followers and political power, his god said in Sura Al Bagharah (2) verse 256: There is no compulsion in religion. And in Sura Al Kahf (18) verse 29 he said to Muhammad: This truth is from God, let anyone who wishes to believe, and let anyone who wishes to disbelieve.

But the god of Islam changed his mind later. When Muhammad found many followers and established an army, his god told him in Sura Al Tawbah (9) verse 33 to make Islam victorious over every other religion.

106

In Sura Al Anfal (8) verse 12 Allah says: I will send terror into the unbelievers' hearts, and you will cut off their heads and even the tips of their fingers.

Again, when Muhammad was weaker in power his god said in Sura Al Bagharah (2) verse 62: Muslims, Jews, Christians and Sabeites who believe in God and the last Day, and do which is right, shall have their reward with their Lord: fear shall not come upon them, neither shall they be grieved. But in Sura Al Bayyina (98) verse 6 says: Christians and Jews and polytheists are the worst among creatures and they go to hell.

Do you see what the god of Islam is doing? First he says to Jews and Christians that they would go to paradise if they follow their own beliefs. But later says that they will go to hell if they do not follow Islam. Does the true God show confusion like this? How can a confused god guide others in the right path?

Even in one Sura, the god of Islam speaks contradicting words. Sura Al-e Imran (3) verse 55 says: I will place Christians above those who do not believe in Jesus, until the day of resurrection. But in the verses 19 and 85 of the same Sura, he says: The true religion with Allah is Islam. No religion other than Islam shall be accepted.

Isn't this shocking that Allah states in one Sura that following Christ is the highest spiritual priority for him, but forgets his comments and says that every one must follow Islam in the same Sura?

In Sura Al Bagharah (2) verse 65 the god of Islam says that he hated those Jews who broke the law of Moses about the Sabbath or Saturday and turned them into monkeys. But on the other hand asks Muslims to put pressure on Jews to leave the Sabbath, become Muslim and follow the Friday prayer.

Isn't this strange? On one hand, the god of Islam forbids Jews to leave their religion, but on the other hand kills them if they do not leave their Sabbath and religion to become Muslim!

Does the honest and all-knowing God one day say that these religions are good, but changes his mind the day after and says that they are bad and their followers must be killed? Absolutely not. The god of Islam did that because he is not the true God and guide.

Allah also misguides Muslims about Jesus

Sura Al-e Imran (3) in verse 55 says: O Jesus I will cause you to die, and will take you up to myself and deliver you from those who believe not. But Sura An Nisa (4) in verses 157 and158 states that Jews did not crucify and kill Jesus but God raised him up unto Himself. Also Sura Al Maeda (5) in verse 117 says that Jesus said to God: ...I was a witness to Jews' actions while I stayed among them; but since You (God) surrendered me to death (فَلَمَّا تَوَفَّيْتَنِي = Falamma Tavaffaytani) You have Yourself watched them ... And Sura Mariam (19) in verse 33 says that Jesus said: the peace of God was on me the day I was born, and will be the day I shall die, and the day I shall be raised to life.

So you see clearly how the god of Islam misleads Muslims about Jesus. On one hand, he says that Jesus died, but on the hand he says that Jesus did not die. Allah's guidance is confusing and cannot be trusted.

Let me give two more examples of Allah's contradictory messages.

In Sura Al Anbiya (21) in verses 34 and 35 Allah says to Muhammad that he did not grant permanent life to any man before Muhammad. Every soul shall have a taste of death ... Sura Al-e Imran (3) in verse 185 says again that every soul shall have a taste of death.

According to these verses everybody before Muhammad, including Moses, Jesus, and others died and Muhammad will die too.

Does the god of Islam know what he is doing? He confirms in suras Al-e Imran, Al Maida, Mariam and Al Anbiya that Jesus died and everybody must die, but in Sura An Nisa he rejects the death of Jesus. This means that the god of Islam is not really sure what he wants to say and what happened to Jesus. What confusion? Can the true God get confused? Absolutely not.

Also, the god of Islam says that Muhammad died but Jesus is alive and in heaven. Jesus is alive and Muhammad is dead! Why didn't Allah ask Muslims to follow Jesus who lives permanently, but asked them to follow Muhammad who is dead permanently?

What has caused the Quran to introduce its god as someone who misguides and takes his righteous followers to hell?

The effect of paganism

Only pagans believe their gods do such things. Muhammad destroyed pagan idols but was unaware that the picture he had of God in his mind was of a pagan god and that he first needed to remove that image from his own mind and heart.

These unethical things I explained are not characteristics of the God that Jesus reveals. The true God is a good guide, who is loving and gives assurance to His followers to be with Him in heaven. You really need to follow Jesus.

Reflection Time 7

1. God is supposed to be the best guide. What are the characteristics of the best guide?
2. How does it feel to be misguided by someone? How about if a god misguides you?
3. Why can't the god of Islam be a good guide?
4. Do we need the genuine spiritual guide in our life on earth? Why?
5. Can we have access to heaven if we do not follow the true God?
6. How important is it to follow the good guide?

Do You Have Peace with God Through Islam?

Is Islam able to establish peace between you and God? Can you say, "I am one hundred per cent on God's side, belong to God's heaven and will not see hell in the future"?

This is what a true belief can do for you. It puts your hands in the hands of God and guarantees your afterlife.

Is Islam that true belief?

Was Islam able to put your hands in the hands of God so far and tell you that your relationship with God is eternal? Can you say that because of Islam you have confidence and peace in your heart now and you do not have any concern about your eternity? Do you know any Muslim in the history of Islam who was able to say, "I am free now, I am saved and I am truly united with God and will be with Him forever."?

You and I know that even Muhammad was unable to testify such a unity with God which could last forever and give him eternal assurance. He said that he never knew what was going to happen to him after death.

God is not interested in a provisional or half-hearted unity. God is perfect and desires a perfect unity. Because, only perfect unity can create eternal peace between God and His people, especially those who claim to be His prophets. Therefore, when a prophet says that he does not know about his afterlife, it means that he is not in unity with God and does not know what the true unity and peace with God is.

This is where I was scared to death about my spiritual life while I was a Muslim. I said to myself that the prophet of Islam was the most pious Muslim. He was the number one in following the instructions of Islam and staying faithful to his god. Despite all his good deeds, he said that his future was unknown to him, whether he would go to heaven or miss it.

I realized that something ought to be wrong in Islam, otherwise, there wouldn't be any uncertainty which terrorized Muslims. Islam means "submission" in Arabic. Muslim means "the one who is submitted to God." Isn't this submission supposed to create assurance in

Muslims about their future? If not, what then is the benefit of submitting to the god of Islam? I asked myself, "Why would I call others to submit to Islam and become ambiguous like me? Why would I follow Islam and allow this uncertainty to torture me daily?" How fortunate was I when these questions started to be parts of my daily life.

Have you had any chance to raise these questions in your mind and come up with any answer? It is vital for you to find a path that rescues you from all kinds of ambiguities, unites you with God and creates eternal peace in your heart. The true God desires you to allow Him to enter your life on earth and give you eternal confidence. Any belief that claims to be from God must be the reflection of God's desire and able to unite you with Him.

Islam has not been able to give you confidence about your future. You desperately need to follow a different belief that is able to unite you with God and establish you in a perfect confidence. Islam is not any different from paganism. Pagans talk exactly like Muslims and say that they also do not know what will happen to them after they die. Pagans are also in fear about their future as much as Muslims are.

What kind of god is the god of Islam who is called compassionate but does not rush to help Muslims with their fear of the future? Muslims pray five times a day, fast for a month each year and do all the other things that they are asked to do, but are still in a terrifying fear about whether they will be able to make their spiritual journey to paradise or will end up in hell. Compassion means sympathy, concern and care. If you are praying and crying to your god everyday to put you on the right path and release you from your fear, why doesn't he free you from your fear and fill your heart with joy and comfort? Something is wrong here. Either God is not compassionate or Muslims are not on a right path. But every religious person in the world believes that God is the source of compassion. If so, then God never delays His compassion to those who cry for His care. Therefore, Islam is not a true religion which delays God's care for people.

When you follow a true belief, God will fill your heart with confidence, peace and joy. Confidence because God is the all-knowing God and will show your future to you; peace because you will be in His arms, in a very safe place and nothing will be able to separate you from His love and care; joy because you will overcome the fear forever.

You do not have any of these in Islam. All you have heard from childhood up until now is that Islam is the last and perfect religion and God is with Muslims. Even though there is not any logical reason in Islam for any one of these claims.

When you say that God is with you but you are not sure about your afterlife, then you can see that Islam is leaving you hopeless about your future. A religion with hopelessness should not be called perfect. Because to be with God means that you are free from fear of going to hell and have one hundred per cent assurance that as you are here with God on earth, you will also be with God in heaven after you die. God is the God of confidence both for this world and the world after. When He is with you now, He gives you the confidence of being with Him in both worlds. If the god of Islam or any other god does not give you confidence for the life after, he cannot be the true God.

The message of Islam is contradicting itself. It says that Muslims are with God in their life on earth, but it is not clear whether they will be with God in the afterlife or go to hell.

Unity and peace with God on earth must lead to eternal unity and peace with God in the afterlife and give complete assurance to people. It is here that the major difference between Islam and faith in Christ shows itself. The Gospel of Jesus Christ says, if you are with God now, you will be with Him forever. But the Quran says, if you are with God now, it is not clear whether you'll be with God in the afterlife or go to hell.

You see that unity with God is the real unity in the Gospel. It establishes a friendship between you and God in such a way which continues to eternity. The real friendship should be deeper, longer and full of confidence. Friendship with the god of Islam is not deep. It is with fear which destroys trust, peace and comfort.

So we can see that the submission to God in Islam is not real but artificial. If it was a true submission, it would not create ambiguity and fear in Muslims about their afterlife, but would give them eternal confidence of being with God.

According to the Gospel of Jesus Christ, if you are submitted to God and united with Him on earth, He never negates His covenant with you but keeps it forever and fills your heart with confidence. Therefore, the unity with God in our lives on earth will take us to heaven in order to be with God forever.

So, when a person asks you whether you have peace with God through Islam, your true response should be "no" since Islam does not give you assurance about your future. Then you need to rush and ask that person to give you advice on what to do to have peace with God and be saved from your fear about your future. You will see the light of heaven in that person if he or she is a follower of Jesus Christ. You will learn how to truly unite with God in every aspect of your life and have peace with Him. You will also learn how to have peace with others.

God is the source of peace. Unity with the source of peace will bring peace into your own life. Then you will become peaceful, a peace-maker and have peace with others too. In other words, if you do not have peace with God, you will not be able to have a genuine peace with people, either in your own family or outside of it. When you unite with God and have peace with God, His compassion becomes the motivating factor in your relationship with others; you therefore become a peace-maker instead of hater. You can say then, "If God is compassionate toward me while I am a sinner, I also need to try my best to be compassionate toward others who are like me."

These compassionate, loving and peace-making attitudes belong to the faith of Jesus Christ not to the Islam of Muhammad. Jesus never hates, curses or kills sinners but always approaches them with kindness and allows kindness to work instead of hatred. For Jesus Christ, love, kindness and peace can change people for good, not hatred and hostility. There is not a single verse in the entire Gospel of Jesus Christ to teach hatred against sinners or people who oppose you. The Gospel never instructs its followers to kill others.

Jesus changed me and millions of others just through his amazing love and kindness. He opened our eyes to see that hatred not only aims at others' lives but also aims at the destruction of peace in our own lives and families.

So, we can see how true unity and peace with God makes us peaceful and paves the way for us to unite with others through love and kindness and live in peace with them. We also can understand now why Islam hasn't been able to establish peace; because, harshness in Islam is stronger than kindness and forgiveness.

My point to you is this: You need to have peace with God now, and that is possible only through Jesus Christ. You also need peace with your family and others. This is also possible only through Jesus Christ.

Are you eager to have peace with God, in your family and in your relationship with others? If you are serious, you need to get your conscience to consider the proven objectives I have been sharing with you.

True peace will not be possible without the leadership of the Prince of Peace

Who is the Prince of Peace? Who do you think the Prince of Peace should be?

He has the heart of God

The Prince of Peace should be someone who has the heart of God in order to be able to approach people as God does.

He respects the rights of others

The Prince of Peace does not practice discrimination but believes in the right of everybody, no matter if they are friends or not, since God has created all with the freedom of choice.

He is generous

As God is so generous and has created the world for all, as He sends His rain for all, the Prince of Peace also must be generous like God in order to win the hearts of His enemies through generosity.

He never rushes to war

Also, the Prince of Peace never rushes to war, since His mission is to bring people to one another through knowledge and understanding in order to establish peace among them.

Now, if you borrow a Gospel from a Christian, read and compare it with the Quran, then you will understand that the Prince of Peace is Jesus.

Seven hundred years before the birth of Jesus Christ, the Prophet Isaiah prophesied about Him like this: For to us a Child is born, to us a Son is given; and the government shall be on His shoulder; and His name shall be called Wonderful, Counselor, The mighty God, The everlasting Father, The Prince of Peace. With the birth of Jesus Christ this prophesy was fulfilled: The Gospel says in the book of Colossians chapter 1 verses 19 and 20 that all the fullness dwelt in Jesus Christ in order to reconcile all things in heaven and on earth to God.

Jesus Christ is the Prince of Peace. He is able to reconcile all to heaven and to one another. Follow Jesus in order to be able to unite with God and have eternal peace with Him.

Reflection Time 8

1. What does it mean to have peace with God?
2. How important is it to have peace with God and in what way does it affect our social life?
3. What role does God play in the establishment of peace?
4. What do we need to do if our belief does not unite us with God?

5. Is there a reason that a trust in Christ unites you with God? If so, what should you need to do then?

Is the Quran the Word of the True God?

How Do We Know if a Book Is from God or Not?

We need to find out whether the words of that book match the characteristics of the true God or not. We need to evaluate the words of that book from every angle. This is what we are going to do with the words of the Quran, a thorough evaluation so that everybody, educated or uneducated, will be able to understand that the Quran cannot be from the true God.

Does the God of Islam Speak Words?

The first assessment is to see whether the god of the Quran can speak words or not. If he cannot, then no one can prove that the Quran is from God.

Only the personal God can have personal words that relate to humanity as personal beings. The god of Islam is a non-relational and impersonal god, he therefore cannot have personal and relational words in order to have a personal relationship with individuals. This means that

Muhammad's god, unlike the God of Moses and other prophets, was unable to have personal communication with him, and he never heard a voice or a word from his god. The Quran, therefore, cannot be from God.

The Bible is the Word of God. Why? Because the God of the Bible is personal and relational, and He expresses Himself with words directly to His people. God spoke to Moses and all other biblical prophets personally, and they heard the words of God from Him personally and with their own ears. The personal experiences of those prophets with God were gathered together as the Bible and as the light for people's life. As a result, the true God must be personal in order to express Himself with words and have a book. The god of Islam is not personal and relational and therefore cannot have a book. The Quran cannot be from the true God.

Does the God of Islam Give Assurance?

The second assessment is to see whether the god of the Quran gives assurance of salvation. If not, then the Quran cannot be from the true God.

The Quran in Suras Luqman (31) and Al Ahqaf (46) clearly says that no one knows what will happen to him in the future. Not only does the Quran provide no such assurance, it also states in Sura Maryam (19) that all righteous Muslims will be sent to hell first for judgment.

The word of the living God must give eternal life to His people, keep them completely away from hell; Since the Quran cannot keep its followers away from hell, it is therefore not the word of God.

Would the true God send His followers to hell even for a short time? Not at all. The Quran states this, because it is not the word of the true God.

The book and words of the true God must be able to build an eternal relationship between God and His followers, but the Quran does not have such authority.

The book of the true God gives you assurance that you are now united with God and saved for eternity; your relationship with Satan and hell is cancelled forever; after you die, you will be directly taken to heaven to have eternal fellowship with God.

The Quran was not even able to give Muhammad, the supreme leader of Islam and the most favored one of Allah, peace and assurance about his future. For this reason, he died without confidence of his salvation. Would the true God disappoint His most favorite one? Absolutely not. The problem is not with God; it is with the Quran. It cannot be from God.

Does the Quran introduce a moral God?

The third assessment is to see whether the god of the Quran is moral or not.

The Quran says that God is a deceiver. Sura Al-e Imran (3) verse 54 and Sura Al Anfal (8) verse 30 say that God is the best of deceivers; Sura Yunus (10) verse 21 says that God is swift in deception; and Sura Al A'raf (7) verse 99 says that no one can feel secure from his deception.

Really? Is the Quran right, calling the true God a deceiver? Absolutely not. The holy, righteous and kind God cannot be a deceiver. The Quran has a fundamental problem by portraying God as a deceiver; it cannot be of the true God.

The Quran says that God is a conspirator. Sura Al Isra (17) in verse 16 says that God inspires people to do immoral things so that he can then have a reason to destroy them.

Does the kind God, loving and compassionate God really become disloyal to His own nature and act like Satan? My goodness! Such comments from the Quran is the clear evidence that it cannot be the word of the true God.

The Quran says that God lies to seize those who oppose Him. Sura Al A'raf (7) in verses 182 and 183 and also Sura Al Ghalam (68) in verses 44 and 45 say: Those who reject our verses we shall gradually seize them in ways when they perceive not my deception (kaydi).

Why then is He acting contrary to His own principle and fighting against the freedom of choice? For sure, the Creator is not intimidated by the freedom of choice He has given to His own created.

Friends, it is very heart-breaking that more than a billion Muslims are following this Quran without knowing that it is speaking against the true God. Does the mighty God need deception and lies to destroy those who oppose Him? Is he so weak that he cannot approach them by speaking the truth instead of using lies and deception? It is shocking that the Quran is bringing the supreme God down to the level of us sinners. On the other hand, God has given people the freedom of choice to accept or oppose him.

The Quran says that God ordained Satan to be a seducer. Sura Al A'raf (7) verse 16 says that Allah corrupted Satan so that he could deceive people. Is it believable that the compassionate God equips a horrible enemy to hurt humanity? Do you believe that a loving mother or father hires an enemy to destroy their child?

It is my prayer and hope that you'll read the Gospel of Christ and the entire Bible to understand that the compassionate God has neither corrupted Satan nor is an opportunist who plans evil things to destroy people. By attributing such an evil and heartbreaking work to God, the Quran cannot be the word of the true God.

The Quran says that Allah planned it so the evil ones could hurt Muhammad. Sura Al An'am (6) in verse 112 says: Likewise, did We make for every

Messenger an enemy - evil ones among men and jinns, inspiring each other with flowery discourses by way of deception. If thy Lord had so planned, they would not have done it: so leave them and their inventions alone.

A true God never cooperates with demons to hurt his beloved prophet. The true God saves from the evil ones. Since the Quran attributes the cooperation of God with demons, it cannot be from the true God.

The Quran says that Allah uses demons for the spread of Islam. On one hand the Quran in Sura Al A'raf (7) verse 27 says: God made the evil ones friends to those without faith. On the other hand, we saw, that he planned jinns to hurt his prophet, Muhammad. Now, the Quran in Sura Al Jinn (72) verses 1 to 2 says: Say O Muhammad: It is revealed unto me that a company of the Jinns gave ear, and they said: Lo! we have heard a marvelous Qur'an, which guides unto righteousness, so we believe in it and we ascribe unto our Lord no partner.

The god of Islam created demons as corrupted beings to follow Satan and become friends with pagans and non-Muslims and also hurt

Muhammad, but he then leads demons to give up friendship with non-Muslims and become friends with his followers for the spread of Islam.

Is this god confused? Whose friend is this god? Does the true God really accept demons to be His genuine followers? Does the true God use demons for the spread of His words? With such strange teachings, the Quran cannot be the book of the true God.

The Quran also attributes the creation of sin to God. Sura Ash Shams (91) in verses 7 and 8 says that God inspired sin in humankind. Sura Al Balad (90) in verse 4 says that God created man in toil and trouble. Suras An Nisa (4) verse 88; Al A'raf (7) verse 178 and Ibrahim (14) verse 4 all say that God leads astray.

The Quran introduces God desperate to initiate immoral and lawless acts or to lead people astray and make them sinners. It introduces God like a person whose heart and mind chase sin. God is not like a human being. He hates sin and misleading acts. The words of the Quran are not only not from God but they also do not lead to God.

Does the God of the Quran believe in equal right?

The fourth assessment is to see whether the god of the Quran believes that all people are equal or not.

The Quran attributes discrimination to God. The Quran says in Sura Al Bagharah (2) verse 65 and Sura Al Maeda (5) verse 60 and Sura Al Anfal (8) verse 55 and Sura Al A'raf (7) verses 175 to 177 and Al Tawba (9) verse 28 that non-Muslims are unclean and animals, but in Sura Al-e Imran says that only Muslims are human, good and clean.

This claim of the Quran can neither be doctrinally and spiritually nor socially and morally true. Why? Doctrinally and spiritually because the Quran itself says that Muslims like all others are sinners. What spiritual reason remains here to make Muslims better than others? Nothing. Socially and morally this claim is ungodly and untrue. How could you put a Muslim, a Christian, a Jew, a Hindu or others, each created by the same God, side by side, say that this one is human but others are animals? The God, who created them, knows that all of them are humankind, but the Quran does not recognize this fact and calls them animals. You see that the Quran does not reflect the heart of God and therefore cannot be from God.

Does the God of the Quran respect the freedom of choice?

The fifth assessment is to see whether the god of the Quran respects the freedom of Choice or not.

The Quran introduces God as someone who thirsts for the blood of His opponents and non-Muslims. More than half of the Quran, more than half of Muhammad's Life Biography and a large portion of Hadiths are about hating and attacking non-Muslims and pouring out their blood for their unwillingness to join Islam. When the prophet and author of Islam spends more than half of his life in attacking his opponents and non-Muslims, what do you then expect his followers to do with their opponents and non-Muslims? What kind of life will non-Muslims have under Islamic government?

The Quran and other Islamic sources reveal to us that they should not have freedom or a comfortable life (Suras 8:39; 48:29; 17:16). The use of force and sword cannot create true heart-felt dedication and submission.

Is it possible to attribute such attitudes to the true and logical God? No. The Quran is not right about God.

The Quran says that God imposes His belief. From the Suras An Nisa (4) verse 89 and An Nahl (16) verse 106 we understand that Muslims are not allowed to use their God-given freedom of choice, leave Islam and follow the belief they want. From the Sura Al Bagharah (2) verse 217 also we understand that Muslims have limitless freedom to invite non-Muslims to their religion and even force them to accept Islam, but it will be worse than being killed if non-Muslims invite Muslims to their religion.

So, Muslims have limitless freedom to spread Islam; non-Muslims cannot, but if they do, they'll be killed. Such a one-way freedom is opportunistic, discriminatory and cruel, and cannot be from the true God. The Quran cannot be from the true God with such teachings.

Does the Quran have a good plan for family?

The sixth assessment is to see whether the Quran has a good plan for family or not.

The Quran encourages the children to disrespect their parents and relatives. Sura Al Tawba (9) verse 23 asks immature children: O you who believe! Choose not your fathers nor your brothers for friends and as guardians if they take pleasure in disbelief rather than faith. Whoso of you takes them for friends, such are wrong-doers.

The Quran not only encourages children to rebel against their parents, but also encourages them to kill their non-Muslims relatives. Sura Al Tawba (9) verse 123 says: O ye who believe! Kill those of the disbelievers who are near to you, and let them find harshness in you, and know that Allah is with those who keep their duty.

Friends, disrespect to parents and killing relatives and others for the sake of their beliefs is invalid for the true God. The Quran cannot be from God based on these comments.

Was the Quran immune from manipulation?

The seventh assessment is to see whether the Quran was manipulated or not.

The Quran says that Muslims changed it. Sura Al Baghara (2) verse 106 says: Whatever a verse do we abrogate or cause to be forgotten, we bring a better one or similar to it. You do not know that Allah is able to do all things? (Nobel Koran) Sura An Nahl (16) verse 101 says: When we change a verse of the Quran in place of another - and Allah knows best what he sends down – disbelievers say: O Muhammad, you are but a forger." Nay, but most of them know not.

From these and other similar verses in the Quran, we understand that as Muhammad's political power was increasing he replaced some of the Quran's previous verses that he did not like with ones he liked. To justify his actions, he told people that God canceled those verses since they were no longer valid for God, and He inspired better verses. Interesting! Is it really possible for God to say he has a better verse than before since every verse he says is perfect because he is the perfect God? Wasn't God aware in eternity that some of his verses would need to be changed in the future so that he could correct them and not allow an imperfect Quran to fall into the hands of Muhammad?

By removing his original words, people doubted and criticized Muhammad and later were killed for their criticism. Why not provide the perfect or final word from the beginning in order to avoid criticism and slaughters? Would the true God confuse people like this and make them hostile to one another? So, you can see that the Quran confirms that some of its verses were made invalid by changing them with better ones. The Quran would never state its verses invalid if it was from the true God.

Hadiths also say that the Quran is retouched and incomplete

In the time of Muhammad and after his death, there were 8 copies of the Quran different from one another in some parts. Muhammad was not sure which was the right one but guessed that the one in the hands of his son-in-law, Ali, could be the one. After Muhammad's death, the division among his successors not only blocked the way for them to authorize Muhammad's desired version but pushed the ruling leader, Othman, to authorize the present Quran which is missing many verses.

Salim-ibn-Gheys (90 Hijra) in his book, The Mystery of Muhammad's Family, says that many verses are missing from the present Quran. Many verses were eaten by a sheep (or a goat); as well as some verses from Suras Al-Nur(24), Al-Ahzab (33) and Al-Hujraat (49) were lost.

If the Quran itself and the ancient Islamic books are saying with one voice that the Quran was retouched, manipulated and that many of its verses are missing, how could the Quran be called the perfect book and from God?

The Bible does not claim to be changed. Sura Al Hijr (15) in verse 91 says that the Quran was retouched and manipulated. Nowhere in the Bible does it say that it was changed or forged.

Muslim leaders and clergies never teach that the Quran was changed or that many of its verses were lost, but easily lie about the books of Christians and Jews saying that they were changed. The Quran's own verses are saying that it was forged. How can then this forged book be from God?

The Quran says in Sura Al An'am (6) verses 34 and 115, and Sura Ynus (10) verse 64: No one can change the words of God, and in Sura Al Hijr (15) verse 9 says: because God will protect it. Now, we understand that the Quran was changed. Therefore, if it was the word of God, nobody could change it.

The Bible and the Gospel of Christ are immune from the problems the Quran has. The God of the Bible does not make His followers captive to sin, Satan and evil ones, but saves them.

Reflection Time 9

1. There are many religions in the world and the followers of each claim that their religion is from God. Do we have the ability to evaluate and see whether a religion is from God or not?
2. Some Muslims say that the Quran is from God because more than a billion Muslims believe that it is from God. What do you think? Is godliness or ungodliness measured by quantity or quality?

3. Do we have any tools to prove that the Quran cannot be from the true God?

4. Do we have a responsibility to discover the true word of God and live by it?

5. If you believe that God is ready to guide you to discovering the truth or helping others to discovering the truth, spend some time in prayer now.

Is Islam really the Last and Perfect Religion?

Islamic leaders and clergies have told Muslims that Islam is the last and most perfect religion. Is it really true? Do they have any logical, doctrinal, philosophical, spiritual or social reason for their claims? What does perfect mean in Islam? Does it mean that Islam has answered the questions of life better than all other religions? Does it mean that Islam has brought new things and more good news which were absent in the religions before Islam? What new perfect things has Islam brought which other religions before Islam did not have so that Islam could claim perfection because of them?

Have you, as a Muslim, ever thought about this question and have come up with any response to it? You know, each one of us is responsible to discover the reasons for our claims, if we want to have confidence personally or be clear in our stand to our family members and others.

Let me tell you briefly in the introduction before explaining my reasons that not only has Islam not brought good new things, but also trampled the good old religious values which were from Abraham, Moses and Jesus. Islam's claim for perfection is nothing but propaganda.

Islam ascribes illogical things to God

The first reason that Islam cannot be the perfect religion is because it ascribes illogical things to God. How does Islam introduce God?

Sura Al Hashr (59) in verses 23 and 24 says that God is holy, peaceful, majestic and wise. But Suras Al-e Imran (3) in verse 54 and Al Anfal (8) in verse 30 say that God is the best of deceivers. Sura Al Baghara (2) in verse 225 and Sura Al-e Imran (3) in verse 28 and Sura An Nahl (16) in verse 106 all say that God sanctioned Muslims to lie in some circumstances.

Can you see the huge contradiction between these verses? On one hand, God is called holy, peaceful, majestic and wise, but on the other hand He is called the best of deceivers. How can God be holy, peaceful, majestic and wise in nature and in the meantime a deceiver too? Can a deceiving god be called majestic and wise?

God is called holy because He hates deception and never deceives. A perfect God does not sanction deception and lying. And, a perfect religion never calls God a deceiver or liar. If you call God a deceiver, it means that he is not perfect. How then can the religion of an imperfect god be called a perfect religion?

Do you call a man perfect if he teaches deception and lying? Do you call his belief a perfect belief? You don't. It is the same with Islam. Since Islam calls god a deceiver and liar, it cannot be a perfect religion.

Islam does not have a perfect response to the question of life

The second reason that Islam cannot be the perfect religion is because it does not have a more perfect response to the questions of life than other religions.

Islam's view of life on earth, judgment day and after life is not any better than other religions which focus on people's deeds concerning salvation. Why then is Islam called more perfect than others? Like all other religions before Islam, Islam also taught Muslims that life on earth was a battleground between good and evil, and salvation was based on continuous purification by good deeds in this world. The teachings about the judgment day and afterlife were also, more or less, similar. Actually, the other religions were better than Islam in this regard. Unlike Islam, they did not teach that imposing religion on others or killing them would lead to paradise.

In comparison with the faith in Christ, Islam is utterly unable to claim perfection over Christianity. The Gospel says that Jesus is sinless, alive, in heaven and is therefore the way to life and heaven. But the Quran never speaks about Muhammad like this.

The Quran actually confirms that Jesus is sinless, alive and in heaven, but never teaches people to follow Jesus for His amazing qualities. Instead, it asks people to follow Muhammad who was sinner, died and is not in heaven. It is crystal clear that Christianity with a sinless and eternally living leader is more perfect than Islam with a sinful leader who died in uncertainty.

So you can see that Islam does not have any better instructions for the purity of life on earth or for the judgment day and afterlife than other religions. Therefore, to call Islam the perfect religion is unwise.

Islam destroyed One-God believing religions

The third reason that Islam cannot be called perfect is because it destroyed all the One-God believing religions in the Arabian Peninsula and the neighboring countries.

The followers of "One-God" believing religions were scattered all over the Arabian Peninsula until Islam was established. These religions were called Abrahamic religions. Sura Al Mo'menun (23) in verses 84 to 90 and Sura Lughman (31) in verses 24 and 25 confirm that many Arab nationals believed in one God. Instead of defending these Abrahamic religions, Islam destroyed them and forced their followers to join Islam.

The religion of Hanif is one example. 'Hanif' was the name of a famous religious group which proclaimed belief in the God of Abraham and rejected polytheistic worship. They were Arabs and from Muhammad's own tribe, Quraish. Muhammad's own life story written by Ibn

Ishagh confirms that Hanifies believed in one God and were the followers of the religion of Abraham. After Muhammad brought Islam, he also called his religion the religion of Abraham (S.3:95; 4:125; 6:161) despite trampling other Abrahamic beliefs.

Idol worshipping was made legalized in Islam for a short time

Hanifies were stronger than Muhammad in their belief about the Oneness of God. They were totally against any kind of idol worship and strongly believed that God was One. But Muhammad asked Muslims to worship three idols while he was in Mecca. He recited a verse in Sura An Najm (53) which was after verse 19. It said that the three idols of al-Lot, the goddess of fertility, al-Uzza, the goddess of power and Manat, the goddess of fate were divine beings, assisting Allah in his work. Upon saying this, Muhammad and his followers bowed down to these idols and worshipped them.

You see that the Quran asked Muhammad and his followers to worship three idols besides God. Muslims in Mecca worshipped these idols under Muhammad's leadership for some time until they migrated to Medina. In Medina Muhammad confessed that this particular verse of the Quran was from Satan. Neither Hanifies nor Christians nor Jews nor Zoroastrians nor Sabeites believed nor practiced idol worship. They rejected it strongly. Their spiritual stand about the Oneness of God was higher than the stand of Muhammad. Not only did Muhammad not appreciate their strong stand about the One God belief, but rather forced them to follow Islam.

How can then Islam with its idol worship and war on One God beliefs be called more perfect than these religions which stayed away from every kind of idol worship? It cannot be.

Anyhow, the idol worshiping verse was removed from the Quran later. After the death of Muhammad, this verse was removed from the Quran by Muhammad's successors. They believed it was from Satan and had to be removed. Islamic ancient scholars have reserved the verse in their books and we still have access to them. The exact verse reads thus: "These are the exalted females, and truly their intercession may be expected".

For what reason did Muhammad sanction idol worship? The major reason for him was political pressure. He lost his encouraging and loyal wife, Khadijah, and his uncle, Abutalib, who were like shields for him against the pressures of idol worshippers whom he criticized in Mecca. As a result, he felt lonely and became more vulnerable to the pressures by the Meccan leaders against him and his Muslim friends. Because of this difficulty he decided to make a slight change to his politics in order to gain the favor of his opponents. For this reason, he legitimized the worship of these three important Qureyshi idols. This caused him to be safe in Mecca for some time until he fled to Medina.

No matter for what reason Muhammad and his followers worshiped idols, in spirituality it is called "creating partners for God". Neither Abraham nor Moses nor Jesus, who were before Muhammad, sanctioned any idol worship, but Muhammad and the Quran sanctioned it, though for a short time.

You see that the Islam of Muhammad was not the most perfect religion among other religions. The claim for perfection was and has been just a political propaganda, though against the heart of God.

Islam sanctions harsher relationship

The fourth reason that Islam cannot be a perfect religion is because of its harsh relationship with people.

I have already covered in my previous talks that Islam sanctions the practice of husbands beating their wives; this was unacceptable to Abraham, Moses and Jesus. Does loving your wife and dealing with her like a human being make your religion a perfect religion or beating her? Islam cannot be the perfect religion.

Islam also sanctions that whatever Muhammad taught, people must blindly obey. This is also not acceptable in the faith of Abraham, Moses and Jesus.

Islam also teaches children to disregard the guardianship of their parents if their parents are not committed to Islam. This attitude cannot be called perfect since it is against the will of God who has created people with the freedom of choice and asks children to honor their parents.

Islam also sanctions that Muslims should wipe out all other religions and force people to follow Islam.

So you see that Islam not only is not better than the previous religions, but instead it is harsher and more imperfect in its approach to families or others.

Islam has stripped itself of perfect values. Conscience calls love, joy, forgiveness, peace, patience, kindness, goodness, gentleness, self-control the perfect things in relationships. Why? Because these behaviors bring people together in order to engage themselves in a creative way to find the best, live in peace together and enjoy each other's company.

But Islam restricts these behaviors. Islam's behavior to its opponents and non-Muslims is torture and destruction. Islam gives more rights to husbands and instructs them to beat their wives. Islam is a threat to the sincere love between one husband and one wife, and instructs a man to have multiple wives. Islam is a threat to moderate Muslims, to non-Muslims and to all who do not align themselves with Islamic values.

With these harsh attitudes Islam cannot be called perfect.

Islam does not give assurance of salvation

The fifth reason that Islam cannot be a perfect religion is because it does not give assurance of salvation.

While assurance of salvation is the most important message of God, Islam lacks it. No Muslim can speak about his or her afterlife with confidence. The god of Islam left even his beloved Muhammad in uncertainty and he died with fear about his future. The god of Islam is not able to save his faithful ones in their life on earth and make their happiness perfect.

No one calls uncertainty and the fear behind it perfect things. The God of a perfect religion must perform His mission perfectly, save people in their life on earth and give them confidence and joy. Isn't it disappointing that the god of Islam assures Muslims one hundred per cent that those who follow Satan will go to hell, but never assures any of his righteous Muslim followers one hundred per cent will go to paradise?

All the followers of the Bible, either a prophet or a simple follower, have the assurance of salvation and going to heaven or paradise.

How then can Islam be more perfect than other religions without the assurance of salvation? It is impossible.

The word "perfect" is a beautiful and encouraging word. But it is so often used aberrantly. Islam is one of those religions that irrationally relates perfect to itself. There are many people and beliefs in this world that call themselves perfect. But it is our personal responsibility to test their claims and discover whether they are sincere in their claims or not. With this, we'll be able to save ourselves and our family from untruth. Insincerity is bad no matter if it is from our own belief, family, forefathers or from others; we need to be aware of it and protect ourselves from it.

You see that committed Muslim leaders from both Sunni and Shia sects have been calling Islam the perfect religion for 1400 years. But their actions have proven that they cannot be sincere in their claim. The leaders of one group call the followers of the other group infidels or Kafirs, which means they have to be wiped out according to the Quran. In the past 1400 years, these two groups have killed millions of each other's followers. If Islam is the perfect religion, why are they unable to extract any perfect relational value from their perfect religion which can obligate them to believe in each other's autonomy, respect one another and live in peace with each other? The problem is not theirs. The problem is at the root of Islam. It is Islam that has sanctioned the looting and destruction of those who think differently. If the Quran was like the Gospel of Jesus Christ, which sanctions the love of opponents and enemies, no Muslim would desire the death of any one. Alas the Quran is not like the Gospel. There is no logical reason to call Islam the last and perfect religion.

Reflection Time 10

1. There are many people in the world who claim that their belief alone is the best and perfect choice for the world. However, only one claim can be true, and the others must be false. How are we able to discover the true claim?
2. Do you have reasons that Islam cannot be the last and perfect religion? Give some examples.

3. Why do both Muslims and non-Muslims need to have logical reason for following their beliefs?
4. How does God feel if someone falsely attributes a religion to Him?
5. If you have discovered that the Path of Jesus Christ is the only true Path, isn't it time for you to put your trust in Him?

Who, Jesus or Muhammad – can be a good leader for you?

Can a sinful or a sinless leader be a good spiritual standard for you? I have asked people similar questions in the last 20 years. Can a sinless or a sinful leader guide you well spiritually? Can a good car run well for you or a faulty car? Will you have a good life with a kind and loving spouse or with an aggressive and unkind spouse?

People always responded that a good leader, spouse, car and every other good thing would make life better. Why? Because God has created us in a way that deep in our hearts we always desire for better and perfect things. We never desire to have a bad family or spouse or house or leader or car or anything else. You never aim to go to the market to buy bad things. You prefer to spend your money for good things. Success is in better things. Successful international companies are successful because of their good standards. They spend huge amount of money to design good and reliable products in order to attract customers, and not to lose them.

In spirituality, it is also the same. Since God is good and perfect, He desires good and perfect things, and expects us to follow His good and perfect model. God wants us to follow a perfect and heavenly leader. God never prefers a sinful leader to a sinless leader. He wants us to make a sinless leader our role model. Even your own Quran in Sura Az Zomar (39) through verses 17 to 18 says: .... announce the Good News to .... Those who listen, and follow the best in it. These verses are saying to you that you need to read the Quran and see who the best standard is and then follow that person.

Let us look at the Quran; if Jesus is sinless and more spiritual than Muhammad, you Muslims then need to follow Jesus as the good example instead of Muhammad.

The Quran says that Jesus is divinely anointed

Sura Al-e Imran (3) in verse 45 and Sura An Nisa (4) in verse 171 say that Jesus is the Christ. What does the word "Christ" mean? Christ means the "Anointed One"; the One Whom God has anointed by His Spirit for His service. When God Himself anoints someone, it means that person is holy and sinless. The Quran nowhere says that God revealed Himself to Muhammad and anointed him personally for his service.

You see that the spiritual position of Jesus Christ is higher than the spiritual position of Muhammad in the Quran. Which one do you need to follow, the One who was with God and touched by Him personally, or the one who did not see God and was not touched by Him?

The Quran says that Jesus is the divine Word of God

Again, Sura Al-e Imran (3) in verse 45 and Sura An Nisa (4) in verse 171 say that Jesus is the Word of God. In religious philosophy, only God is called "the Word". The "Word" is the philosophical name for God. If you ask the Muslim philosophers "What is God?" their responses will be, "He is the Word." Interestingly the Quran describes Jesus in the same way that God is described in Islamic philosophy. In other words, when the Quran says that Jesus is the Word of God, it means that "He has the nature of God".

Let me tell you how God as the "Word" works among people. When it comes to practice, the

God the Word describes Himself in two ways. One way is through the written words, but the second way is through the personal revelation. "Through the written words" means that God the Word describes Himself through the heavenly Scriptures. "Through the personal revelation" means the Word (God) reveals Himself personally. Through the written words, God describes His characteristics and His plan for us in order to prepare us for having a personal encounter with Him. But the personal revelation of God is to reveal His glory to us personally in order to draw our attention to Him and prepare us to invite Him with His written words into our hearts. In other words, if God does not reveal Himself and does not reside in our hearts, His words will not be practical in our lives.

Let me give you an example and make it more understandable: It is the personal presence of your worldly father that makes his instructions relevant to you as his child. If your father hides himself from you, then the lack of intimate relationship makes his instructions impractical for an intimate life. This is the same in your relationship with God. If God does not have an intimate relationship with you, His distance will make his words distant from you.

Since the Quran says that Jesus was touched by God personally and also calls Jesus by the personal Name of God, it means that Jesus is the Only One who can bring the written Word of God or the Holy Scriptures into your heart and save you. This is the highest heavenly title that the Quran attributes to Jesus but not to Muhammad.

Muhammad is therefore unable to make the written words of God relevant to your life. Muhammad is not the personal Word of God, therefore he will not be able to build an intimate relationship between you and God. That's why he said that he was not sure about his own future and was also unable to assure his followers. Secondly, unlike Jesus, he did not have a personal relationship with God and therefore would not be able to describe God to people as Jesus did.

So we see that according to the teachings of the Quran, Jesus is introduced by the name of God and has tremendously higher spiritual position than Muhammad. You Muslims need to follow Jesus instead of Muhammad.

The Quran says that Jesus is the Spirit of God

Sura An Nisa (4) in verse 171, Sura Maryam (19) in verse 17 and Sura Al Anbiya (21) in verse 91 say that Jesus is the Spirit of God.

Some Muslim scholars say incorrectly that this is not the Spirit of God but a spirit or an angel from God who was given birth by Mary. This is actually against the teaching of the Quran. The Arabic Quran says in all places that God sent his Spirit to Mary but not one of his spirits or angels. God's Spirit and one of God's angels or spirits are two different things. If God wanted to send his angel, he would clearly say that He sent his angel. He would not talk ambiguously. Therefore, those who translate this as one of God's angels are manipulating the words of their own Quran.

Suppose it was an angel who came to Mary and was born as Jesus Christ. Still the spiritual position of Jesus Christ would be higher than the spiritual position of Muhammad. Because an angel is always with God, lives eternally and knows everything about the unseen world. But Muhammad says in Sura Al A'raf (7) in verse 188 that he does not know anything from the unseen world. So, Jesus knows everything of God, but Muhammad doesn't. We also know that Muhammad died and he is not in heaven.

So, we can see whether the phrase "the Spirit of God" is translated as an angel or translated as it is in its Arabic form, in both cases they reveal that the spiritual position of Jesus Christ is higher than the spiritual position of Muhammad. It will therefore be good for you to follow the One who has a higher spiritual position than Muhammad.

The Quran says that Jesus is creator and healer

Sura Al-e Imran (3) in verse 49 and Sura Al Maeda (5) in verse 110 say that Jesus created a bird, raised the dead and healed the blind.

According to the Quran, Jesus is still alive and in heaven. Since He is alive, He still has power to create, to heal and to raise people from the dead, but Muhammad did not have such heavenly powers. All people need someone to heal and give life to them. We must honor a life-giving person more than the one who does not have such power. Wouldn't it be good if Jesus were your leader and you had assurance of healing and life? It would be good for you to follow Jesus.

The Quran says that Jesus is holy and sinless

Sura Maryam (19) in verse 19 says that Jesus Christ is sinless and holy. No one is called sinless in the Quran except Jesus. The Quran calls all other prophets and Muhammad sinners. Some Muslims believe that Muhammad is sinless. Such a belief is against the teaching of the Quran.

See what the Quran says about Muhammad: Sura Muhammad (47) in verse 19 says to Muhammad: .... ask forgiveness for your sin and for believing men and believing women. Sura Al Fath (48) in verse 2 says: Allah may forgive you Muhammad of your past and future sin. Sura Ghafir (or Al Mo'men) (40) in verse 55 says [to Muhammad]: And ask forgiveness of your sin. In Sura Al A'raf (7) verse 188 Muhammad says: ... If I had knowledge of God, I should have multiplied all good, and no evil should have touched me.

If Muhammad was a sinless person, he would never speak like this. He is confessing that evil touched him and caused him to sin. All these verses are saying that Muhammad was a sinner. Also, Sura Loghman (31) in verse 34 and Sura Al Ahghaf (46) in verse 9 say that Muhammad was not sure of his salvation after death. This means that Muhammad was not sure that his sins were forgiven, otherwise he would not worry about the future.

You see that the Quran calls Muhammad a sinner, but Jesus righteous, holy and sinless. A sinner cannot guide you to holiness and righteousness. You need to follow the sinless Jesus instead of following sinful Muhammad.

The Quran says that Jesus is alive and in heaven

Sura Al-e Imran (3) in verse 55 and Sura An Nisa (4) in verse 158 say that Jesus ascended into heaven. But Muhammad died and according to Sura Maryam (19) verses 66 to 72 he is not in heaven.

The Quran itself is saying to you that Jesus is alive and in heaven but Muhammad died and is not in heaven; he is waiting for judgment in the Last Day. That's why we all need to follow the One who is alive and in heaven. Only He can lead us to heaven, because He is in heaven.

You see that even the Quran reveals that Jesus is greater than Muhammad. If you read the Gospel of Jesus Christ you will be fully amazed. Follow Jesus Christ.

Reflection Time 11

1. Some Muslims say that though Jesus is described as sinless and more spiritual than Muhammad in the Quran, but God decided to give the completion of His mission on earth to Muhammad. What do you think? Does God entrust the completion of His work to a sinner instead of one who is sinless?

2. Suppose God gives His final work to a sinner rather than a sinless one. Doesn't this mislead people into thinking that God's preference is not always purity but sinfulness too? Wouldn't his cause people to follow every leader they want since God does not have an absolute standard?

3. Logically speaking, isn't it good to follow a sinless spiritual leader as our role model instead of a sinful one?

4. The Gospel exists in Muslims' languages in the world. Don't you think that Muslims need to read the Gospel personally and become captivated personally by the characteristics of Jesus Christ?
5. Pray for Muslims to become courageous for reading the Gospel.

Leadership in Islam Is Chaotic

As you are aware, the discussion about everything in life without referring to our consciences may lead us to negligence, bigotry or rigidity. This is also true about leadership. For this reason, I would like to raise a few awakening questions and find responses for them before entering our discussion today so that we can continue with open minds and hearts.

What kind of leadership do you like to see in your family or society?

A humble leader who sees himself as a servant of his family and society, does not discriminate between male and female, insider and outsider, and who tolerates criticism? Or a leader who is a dictator and discriminator, does not tolerate criticism, oppresses or destroys his opponents?

In my own personal experiences, years of study about many cultures and my journey to many parts of the world all tell me that people love to have a good and humble leader. I am sure that your conscience also confirms this. Do you like a leader who treats others, no matter what their beliefs, nationality or race, equally with his followers or the leader who discriminates against others or even destroys them if they do not follow him or his beliefs? Again, our consciences tell us that a good leader stays away from all kinds of discrimination.

A Muslim leader not only discriminates between husband and wife, male and female, insider and outsider but also has legitimate rights to destroy if they do not follow him blindly. Let me reveal the instructions of Islam that give legitimate rights to a leader to discriminate.

Discrimination within the family

Sura Al Baghara (2) in verse 228 and Sura An Nisa (4) in verse 34 say that ladies belong to an inferior class. Sura An Nisa (4) in verses 11 and 176 says that daughters get half the inheritance than sons get. Sura Al Baghara (2) in verse 282 says that two ladies' witness is equal to one man's witness. Sura Al Ahzab (33) in verse 33 says that ladies must abide at home quietly and should not go out. Sura An Najm (53) in verse 2 tells us that Muhammad is the owner of his wives. Sura An Nisa (4) in verse 34 and Sura Sad (38) in verse 44 tell us that husbands can beat their wives. There is no doubt that those who are committed to the

Quran put these family discriminations into practice in their daily lives.

A male leader of the family has the right to kill his family members

Sura Al Tawba (9) in verse 123 says: You who believe (Muslims), kill any disbelievers who are close to you, relatives and neighbors, so that they may find out how harsh you are. Allah is with those who are pious.

This means that a pious Muslim has religious rights to fight with his immediate and extended family members, with friends and neighbors and even kill them if they do not join Islam. So, a Muslim leader has the right to destroy the life of his family members, friends and neighbors for the sake of his religion.

Discrimination within the society

We have looked into the verses from the Quran that legitimize discrimination within the family. Now let us look into discrimination within the society.

Sura Al Ahzab (33) in verse 36 says: It is not for a believer, man or woman, when a matter has been decided by Allah and his apostle to have any choice in his or her decision. So, according to the Quran, a Muslim leader has a sovereign right in his leadership and others cannot question him. Sura Al Mujadila (58) in verse 20 says: Those who resist Allah and His Apostle will be among those most humiliated.

In comparative leadership studies, this is called One-Way leadership or dictatorship in which a leader expects his followers to follow him blindly.

The slide you see below compares the leadership of Muhammad with the leadership of Jesus. The one headed arrow is an indication to a non-participative leadership style while the two headed arrows indicate to an open leadership that necessitates the participation of followers or delegates. So you see that communication in Muhammad's leadership is a one-way communication, from top to bottom, and people do not have the right to give their opinions, but the leadership style of Jesus is participative and people have the complete freedom to express themselves to each other and to their leaders.

Comparing the Leadership of Muhammad and Jesus

Muhammad's Leadership

↓One Way Communication↓

Followers   Followers

_____

Jesus' Leadership

↕Multiple Communications↕

Followers   ↔   Followers

Let me give you an example of severity in Islamic leadership. The Hadith 330 in the Book of 89 and Volume 9 of Bukahri says that Muhammad said: "I was about to order for collecting firewood and then order someone to pronounce the Adhan[7] for the prayer and then order someone to lead people in prayer and then I would go from behind and

_____

[7] The call from a minaret for united prayer.

burn the houses of men who did not present themselves for the prayer."

Muhammad as the highest authority in Islamic leadership preferred to leave his obligatory community prayer behind to go and burn the houses of those men who were absent in the community prayer. A contemporary Muslim leader also has obligation to follow the leadership model of Muhammad with the same severity against those who do not pray. The leadership in Islam is based on one-way dialogue

You see that you are free to join a Muslim leader but are not free to criticize him, leave him or be his opponent. Islam has sanctioned humiliation, invasion and death for those who want to use their God-given freedom and oppose or leave their leaders. A Muslim leader is against freedom. Those who criticize a Muslim leader have a painful life

Sura Al Anfal (8) in verses 6, 12, 13, 22 and 31 calls those who criticize a leader deaf, mute and the worst of beasts; their finger tips and heads must be chopped off. There are 146 references to Hell in the Qur'an. Only 9 references are for moral failings, murder, theft, etc. The remaining 137 are for those who criticize Muhammad or do not follow him. It is for this reason that a Muslim leader can make the lives of his opponents like hell.

Discrimination against non-Muslims

The lives of non-Muslims become even worse under Islamic leadership. Sura Al-e Imran (3) in verse 110 tells that Muslims are better than non-Muslims. Sura Al A'raf (7) in verses 176 and 177 and Sura Al Anfal (8) in verse 55 tell that those who do not join Islam are dogs and the worst of beasts. Sura An Nisa (4) verse 89 says: Do not choose friends from infidels till they leave their homes and run; do not take them as friends if they turn back but kill them wherever you find them. Sura Al Fath (48) in verse 29 tells that Muhammad is the apostle of Allah; and those who are with him are strict with unbelievers, but compassionate amongst each other. Non-Muslims will therefore not be safe in the hands of a Muslim leader.

A Muslim leader is instructed to create problems for other nations

Sura Al-e Imran (3) in verse 85 says: No religion other than Islam shall be accepted. Sura Al Ahzab (33) in verse 27 says: Allah gave Muslims the lands, dwellings and wealth of non-Muslims for a heritage – even a land on which Muslims had never set foot: for the might of Allah is equal to all things. Sura Al Anfal (8) in verse 39 says: So fight non-Muslims until there is no more disbelief in the whole world and all submit to the religion of Allah alone.

You see that a Muslim leader has the legitimate right from Islam to be an adversary to the world. So a committed Muslim leader has the right from Islam not only to disregard the freedom of his own family, people and the world, but also to impose his beliefs on others.

In comparison with all other leadership styles in the world, Islamic leadership is the most underdeveloped and irresponsible leadership style. Why is leadership in Islam underdeveloped and irresponsible? Because, responsibility necessitates mutual respect for freedom of choice in relationships. But as we learned from the verses of the Quran, no one has any freedom of choice when it comes to Muhammad's decisions.

Quality does not qualify a leader in Islam but power

In the Hadith of Dawud Number 2527 of Book 14 Muhammad said that war for Allah is compulsory for every Muslim under every Muslim leader, whether pious or not; the prayer is also obligatory for Muslims behind every Muslim leader, whether he is pious or impious even if he commits a grave sin. You can see that people are disarmed of their responsibility to avoid rulers who commit grave sins.

This is not a quality leadership but a power thirsty leadership that forces people to follow without question. So it is the power, not the quality that qualifies a leader for leadership in Islam.

The thirst for power causes a leader to ignore the capability of people to make decisions and run their own lives. The thirst for power blinds a leader from understanding that humans can improve their conditions only through reason and rationality. The thirst for power blinds a leader for understanding that he himself needs the opinions and experiences of others for his own well-being and improvement. The thirst for power makes a leader unable to understand that he must be accountable to his society which has placed him in that position. There is no doubt the thirst of a leader for power will ruin the desire for a sincere friendship in his society, but will lead to distrust and fear. Fear will also close the door to the sharing of ideas. People won't be able to trust each other, and thereby the door will be closed to creativity and progress. That's why there is no creativity or progress in any Islamic country that is run by committed Muslim leaders. The lack of creativity will also close the door to prosperity and comfort.

A Muslim leader expects only submission

The word "Islam" means submission in Arabic. Whether you like Islam or not, you have no choice but to submit in every aspect, spiritually, socially or politically. If you do not, you are then ranked an infidel, must be dealt with according to the instructions of the Sharia which is privation of equal rights, or persecution if needed or losing your life.

Leadership in Christ is based on love, kindness and harmony

Leadership in Jesus Christ is different from Islamic leadership in every aspect. Leadership in Christ is to value the presence of all, friends and others. Friends and others are the same in the eyes of the God that Christ reveals (read Matthew 5:43-48; Galatians 3:28; Exodus 23:9; 22:21). Love and kindness are the supreme priorities of leadership in Jesus Christ (read 1 John 4:19).

Leadership in Christ is not to dominate, but a door to a better and successful life so that everybody is encouraged to step forward and work with others in love, kindness and harmony. Leadership in Christ establishes people, both friends and strangers, in confidence so that all can be productive. It is a participative leadership and everyone can give his opinion, either in opposition or in favor, to the leader (2 Timothy 2:24-25; Deuteronomy 18: 22; Isaiah 1: 18) since the goal is not enmity but to find the key factors for success.

Leadership in Christ is servant-hood

The Gospel opposes totalitarianism but supports moderation and freedom. Jesus said: Whoever desires to become great among you, let him be your servant .... the son of man did not come to be served, but to serve, and to give His life a ransom for many (Matt. 20:25-28). Jesus also said: If I then, your Lord and Teacher, have washed your feet, you also ought to wash one another's feet (John 13:14, ESV).

Leadership in Christ is for peace with all

As I have mentioned continually, the Gospel says: There cannot be Jew nor Greek, there is neither bond nor free, there is no male nor female; for you are all one in Christ Jesus (Galatian 3:28, KJV). It also says: Make every effort to live in peace with all men (Hebrew12:14, NIV); The Lord's servant must not quarrel; instead, he must be kind to everyone, able to teach, not resentful. Those who oppose him he must gently instruct, in the hope that God will grant them repentance leading them to a knowledge of the truth (2Timothy 2:24-25, NIV); Whoever does not love does not know God, because God is love (1 John 4:8, NIV). These are the qualities of leadership in Jesus Christ.

Which leader do you desire to follow deep in your heart?

An Islamic leader whose priority is blind submission, and if you do not submit you lose everything. Or the leadership in Christ where the leader is asked to be your servant and people have the freedom to give their opinions, either in favor or in opposition, without any problem? Jesus Christ is unique in every aspect, including leadership. Follow His leadership.

Reflection Time 12

1. How powerful are people's beliefs in shaping their life values, including leadership?
2. What are the characteristics of the best leader?
3. Do you love to be a good leader (father or mother) for your family and to have a good leader?
4. How critical is it to find a belief that has the best leadership values and role model?
5. What are the benefits of a humble leader?
6. Do you find the best model of leadership in Jesus Christ or not? Why?
7. How vital is it to follow Jesus Christ if He is the best model of leadership? In what ways

would it affect your relationship with your family members and others?

The Sharia of Islam or the Love of Christ - which is the better model?

There is no doubt that every belief in the world affects the lives and relationships of its followers and the establishment of the law in that society. Islam also has affected the life, relationship and the law of Muslim societies through its "Sharia" which is based on the Quran, Muhammad's life and the sayings of Muhammad and his successors.

Sharia reveals the way of life for each Muslim. It instructs Muslims that the example of Muhammad must rule nations and make them Islamic in every aspect. At family level father or husband is called to establish the codes of Sharia, and at state and global level government is responsible for enforcing the principles of Sharia. Examples of these principles are laws about food, polygamy, the age of marriage, disobedience, criticism, level of punishment, alcoholic beverages, adultery, non-Muslims, Jihad, etc.

The central focus of Sharia is to Islamize every thing and person

Sharia's motive is conditional. You are not safe if you do not follow Islam. But the central emphasis in the Path of Jesus Christ is the unconditional love. This unconditional love impacts the lives, relationships and the laws of the followers of Jesus Christ in order to prepare them for peace with others.

The Gospel of Christ says in the book of 1 Corinthians chapter 13 verses 1 and 2: If I speak in the tongues of men and of angels, but have not love, I am a noisy gong or a clanging cymbal. And if I have prophetic powers, and understand all mysteries and all knowledge, and if I have all faith, so as to remove mountains, but have not love, I am nothing. (ESV)

Dear friends, the book of such amazing love and kindness is rejected by Muslim leaders with the excuse that the name of Muhammad does not exist in it. They do not know that such love from the true God is better than the names of all prophets.

I am going to give some examples from the Sharia of Islam in comparison with the Gospel of Christ. Then you yourself will be glad to know why the name of Muhammad could not be in the Gospel.

Which one, the Sharia of Islam or the Gospel of Christ, honors the family best

Family must be the most important unit for God since He started the world with a family, Adam and Eve. But in the Sharia of Islam, a husband is greater than his wives and can beat them. Sura Al Baghara (2) in verse 228 says that men have a degree of advantage over their wives. It is because of this masculine advantage that Sura An Nisa (4) verse 34 and Sura Sad (38) verse 44 sanction that men have the right to beat their wives. Sura An Nisa (4) in verses 15 and 16 even says that men have the right to lock their wives in a room for immorality until they die. But for the same immorality, men get some slashes and walk free.

Why does the Quran sanction man's superiority to his wives and give him the right to beat his wives and even kill her? The reasons of the Quran are:

Sura An Nisa (4) verse 34 says that Allah has given men more strength to dominate women and force them to obedience. Various versions of the Quran say in Sura Al Ahzab (33) verse 23 that among Muslims, men are the only ones who have been true to their covenant with God. In other words, women cannot keep their covenant with God and always need to be corrected by men.

Muhammad the prophet of Islam also gives his own reason on why men have more rights than women? He said in the Hadith of Al Bukhari Number 301, in the book of 6 and Volume 1 that Women are lacking in intelligence.

What DO YOU think? Do you really think that men keep their covenant with God better than women? Doesn't this mean, "Don't trust your mother and sisters?"

According to the Quran, you, as a boy or man, carry two times more value than your sister or mother in witnessing or receiving inheritance. This means that if your mother or sister informs you of something, you should not trust her unless another lady witnesses the same. But if your father or brother or a man witnesses something, he can be trusted. Imagine that in a society there is only trust in men but not in women!

Famous Islamic scholars call women crooked

The Hadith number 113 of Bukhari in Volume 7 says that Woman was created from man's rib, crooked. This crookedness is inherent and incurable. Muslim's Hadith number 3467 in Book of 8 says that Woman has been created from a rib and will in no way be straightened for you; so if you wish to benefit by her, benefit by her while crookedness remains in her. And if you attempt to straighten her, you will break her, and breaking her is divorcing her. Davud's Hadith number 2155 in Book 11 Says that Muhammad said: If one of you marries a woman or buys a slave, he should say: "O Allah, I ask You for the good in her, and in the disposition You have given her; I take refuge in You from the evil in her, and in the disposition You have given her." ....

Hadith number 219 of Bukhari, in Book 88 and Volume 9 says: When Muhammad heard the news that the people of Persia had made the daughter of king Khosrau their Queen (ruler), he said, "Never will succeed such a nation as makes a woman their ruler. "

Since Muhammad and the Quran introduced women as evil beings, what will commentaries say about women?

Sura Al Room (30) in verse 21 says that women are created for men. Razi (856 AD) a Sunni philosopher in his commentary book At-Tafsir al-Kabir while commenting on this verse says: "created for man" is proof that a woman is an animal. Hadi Sabzevari (1797) a Shia philosopher in his commentary Sadr al-Mota'aleghin says : women are truly and justly among the mute animals. They have the nature of beasts.

It is so sad that these gentlemen were called philosophers and received much honor from their contemporary governments.

The Gospel of Christ does not say such heart-breaking things about girls and women.

Husband and wife are equal in the eyes of God of the Gospel

The Gospel says in the book of Galatians chapter 3 verse 28 that husband and wife have the same value for God. In the book of Ephesians chapter 5 verses 25 and 28 it says that a man must love his wife as his own body. In the book of Colossians chapter 3 verse 19 it says: Husbands, love your wives, and be not bitter against them. (KJV) And in the book of 1 Peter chapter 3 verse 7 it says that wives are the heirs of God's grace with their husbands. Husbands' prayers will not be accepted if they do not understand and honor their wives.

This has been a comparison of the treatment of women in Islam to the treatment of women in Christianity. Which one do you think should be called the perfect religion?

Now let us see the more shocking treatment of the family in the Sharia of Islam.

Sharia asks children to disobey their guardians

Sura Al Tawba (9) in verse 23 is telling us that Muslim children should not accept the guardianship of their fathers or brothers if the guardians love other values more than the values of Islam.

You know that mature children of a family do not need guardianship, but the immature ones. Here in this verse the Quran is asking the immature children to disobey their guardians if they are not good Muslims. Will you be happy if someone encourages your children to disregard your fatherhood or guardianship? This is what the Quran does.

As you are aware, there is a loving bond even between animals and their young, just as there is between parents and their children. Even the most ungodly person loves his children. This is because God has created us to love each other. This loving bond is from God. The true God never teaches children to ignore their parents.

You see how the Sharia is against the inherent love which is from God. If the Sharia treats its own Muslim family members unkindly, what do you think it will do to non-Muslims? Let us see the instruction of the Sharia of Islam about non-Muslims.

Sharia does not treat non-Muslims as human

The Quran calls non-Muslims unclean. This is why non-Muslims who work in Saudi Arabia should stay 24 kilometers away from Mecca.

Again this has been why some Muslims had no choice but to wash their hands after shaking hands with non-Muslims. Or, if they offered food and water to non-Muslims, to wash their plates and glasses in an Islamic way. I was taught from childhood, if we touched a non-Muslim we had to wash ourselves in an Islamic way to purify ourselves.

The Quran also calls non-Muslims worst of beasts, dogs, pigs, monkeys and donkeys. Calling others as animals is treason to God, to humanity and even to Abraham who is called the father of both Jews and Arabs: Muhammad and Jews are both the offspring of Abraham. How can God, who loved Abraham, say to his face that his offspring are animals? How could the grandchild, Muhammad, tell his grandfather Abraham that his grandchildren from Isaac were animals, only the grandchildren from Ishmael were humankind? Isn't this disrespectful to Grandfather Abraham who loves his all grandchildren? By calling Jews animals you are indeed saying to the grandpa that he produced animals.

Sharia calls non-Muslims animals in order to legitimize murdering them

Sura Al Anfal (8) in verse 39 says: Slaughter non-Muslims until there is no more disbelief in the whole world and all submit to the religion of Allah alone. This is the motivation behind much of the terrorism towards non-Muslims taking place in some Islamic countries. The Quran calls non-Muslims Kafirs and says that they may be hated, mocked, deceived, plotted against, enslaved, tortured and killed if they do not follow Islam.

These kinds of attitudes and action are fully rejected in the Gospel of Christ. The loving, compassionate and kind God does not ask His followers to persecute others for the sake of their beliefs. Friends, there is not a single verse in the entire Gospel of Jesus Christ to encourage hatred or murder. You cannot find any verse like that. Why? Firstly, because God values the life of His creatures so much. Secondly, since we have not created people, we therefore do not have any right over their lives.

It is not possible to create peace in the family or in society with hatred and hostility of Sharia, but it is possible with the love and kindness of Christ. So the love of Christ is the better model for human relationships, not the Sharia of Islam.

Reflection Time 13

1. Can we establish a long-lasting friendship in our family or with others through harshness, discrimination or hostility?
2. How would it affect our children if we followed Sharia and become harsh to our spouses?
3. Can a person become a genuine follower of God or of a prophet by force and violence?
4. Does God need force to convince people since He is the source of all wisdom and can convince people with reason?
5. Does God need force to make followers despite giving freedom of choice to people?
6. Why does the love of Christ surpass the principles of the Sharia?
7. Do you feel responsible to share about the love of Christ with other?

Humanity Needs Friends Not Enemies

Do you agree with me? If you do, we then need to find out how and in what ways we can make long-lasting friends.

As it is not pleasant for us to have enemies, it is also not pleasant to others if we become their enemies. It is very clear that we cannot make genuine friends with anger, hatred, hostility, deception, lying or any other unethical means. Unethical means are the means of war against the rights of others. When we breach the rights of others, we won't be able to build friendship with them. Friendship necessitates respect, kindness, sacrifice, forgiveness, patience and self-control.

All these are saying to us that we need to stay away from any person or belief that teaches us hatred, anger, violence or any unethical behavior against others who do not think our way. We need to stay away from them because not only do they ruin friendship in our societies but in our own families too.

Hating others is not just hating others

By planting a seed of hatred in your heart, you're planting it in your own family also. Let me give you an example. The prophet of Islam encouraged Muslims to hate pagans and the followers of other religions. That hatred motivated them to force all non-Muslims in the Arabian Peninsula to become Muslims and also to kill those who did not want to join Islam. All of Saudi Arabia was fully made subject to Islam, and there were no non-Muslims left over whom to practice their hatred. Did that hatred disappear? No. The hatred which was planted in the hearts of Muslims against non-Muslims in the early mission of Islam, bore the fruit of hatred in Islam's own children, divided Muhammad's own family, created hostility among them and the future Muslim generations. That hatred created Sunni and Shia which have been shedding the blood of each other for 1400 years since the rise of Islam.

Isn't it strange? You think that by planting the seed of hatred in your heart against others you will only hurt others, but that is not the whole case. You will hurt yourself and your own family too. Hatred makes others antagonistic and also

192

poisons the hater. That's why Jesus Christ says in His Gospel that we should not hate even our enemies, but love them and pray for them.

· Unfortunately, Islam opens the door wide to hatred and violence at every level of relationship among Muslims and thereby becomes a threat to sincere love and respect.

Beating wife is bad for every one in the family

When a Muslim follows the order of the Quran and beats the mother of his children, the children of that mother are not going to learn love and respect from the hostility of their father but bitterness and anger. That anger and hostility will impact children's behaviors and make them unfriendly to one another and others.

If the Quran taught families a true love, that true love between a husband and a wife would not make one superior to the other, but make them one unified body so that they could love each other as their own body despite differences. Hands, legs, eyes, all other members of one body are different from one another. They carry the same value for the body, love and complement each other and work in harmony in order to make a unified and healthy body. The members in a family must be similar to the members in a body. If a husband beats his wife his family cannot be a healthy and loving family. Therefore, you will not be able to establish a loving, caring and successful family unless you adopt and practice the best family values. This means that you need to start to become nicer, more respectful, kind and forgiving to your spouse who has a significant role in running the family with you.

The truth is that only Jesus Christ can give you the best family values and form such a unity. Marriage from the viewpoint of the Gospel of Jesus Christ is a model of such unity between a husband and a wife which reveals their heavenly excellence. For Jesus Christ, marriage is not to make a man superior to his wife, but a god-like man who becomes more compassionate and loving to his wife as he is to his own body.

We saw in an earlier episode how renowned Muslim scholars belittle women in the family and equate them with animals. If the Quran did not ask them to beat their wives, they wouldn't end up calling their wives animals, justifying their ugly behaviors.

In your family, you need friends not enemies. With superiority to your wife or beating her, you will not be able to make a friend. For this reason, you need to leave the Quran and follow the Gospel of Jesus Christ.

Polygamy is the cause of disunity and hostility

The Quran also becomes the cause of disunity and hostility in a family with legalizing polygamy. When you follow the order of the Quran and have more than one wife, that polygamy will create disharmony and jealousy among the members of your family.

As a Muslim you may say, "Yes, polygamy creates disharmony simply when the husband is unable to behave justly or establish justice among his wives; if a husband is just, there will not be any problem." Really? Muslims believe that Muhammad was fully equipped to establish justice in his family. If this were the case, why wasn't there harmony between him and his wives?

Let me give you an example from the Quran: Sura Al-Tahrim (66) speaks about the existing disharmony between Muhammad and his wives. You see that even the most just man in Islam was unable to have a happy and loving life with polygamy.

From the beginning of creation, God knew that polygamy would not create love and friendship. Otherwise, He would have created many Eves for Adam. But He created one wife for Adam and created one husband for Eve. I myself have come from a polygamous family, and I have also witnessed many other polygamous Muslim families whose problems were way more than the problems of the Muslim families with one wife. Polygamy creates disharmony and hostility. This not only creates problems between spouses, but also within family relationships.

We need to attach ourselves to the Gospel of Jesus Christ which brings harmony, love and friendliness in a family when one husband and one wife unite with one another and love each other whole-heartedly.

Teaching children to disrespect their guardians is poison to friendship

The Quran also creates enemies by encouraging children to become disrespectful to their fathers and disregard their parenthood. These are not positive values. Children need to be respectful to their parents.

The Quran in Sura Al Tawba (9) verse 23 says that you should not be respectful to your father if he is not committed to Islam. This order of the Quran is not going to build a healthy family. Your father deserves your respect. He has worked hard, fed you day and night so that you could grow and become a father or mother yourself. How can you expect your children to be kind to you while you reject your own father simply because he is not committed to your belief and does not think or believe your way? On the other hand, how can you expect others to be friendly to you while you are hostile to your own father who is closer to you than others?

Let me raise another question. Wasn't your father created by God with freedom of choice to choose any belief he likes? You don't have the right to be disrespectful to your father. Respect him no matter what he believes. Fatherhood and motherhood are so much important to God of the Bible. God uses the example of a father and a mother in the Bible and tells us that He loves us like a mother or a father. The true God never asks you to disrespect your father and become his enemy.

You need a friend in your family not an enemy. For this reason, you need to avoid this instruction of the Quran and respect the freedom of your family members for whatever belief they want to choose. Actually, you will act against God, if you do not value others' God-given freedom but impose your views or beliefs on them.

Killing others for the sake of their beliefs close the door for friendship

Also, when you follow the order of the Quran and kill your non-Muslim relatives and neighbors, it means that you are closing the door to friendship but opening it wide to hatred, revenge and hostility. Such a hatred never ends. The hostility between you and others will never end, unless you and your family leave Islam, follow a loving belief and love and respect your neighbors, as yourself. Otherwise, your unfriendly behavior will impact the neighborhood negatively and will close the door to sincere friendship and care.

Thinking yourself better than others is an obstacle to friendship

The Quran also teaches that you are better than others. This teaching will never allow you to have a sincere friend in your life. The Quran says in Sura Al-e Imran (3) verse 110 that Muslims are better than non-Muslims.

How can you become better than a Jew or a Christian or others, if you are also a sinner like them? How can a sinner be better than other sinners? Sinners are all the same in the eyes of God. On the other hand, true friendship necessitates humility, kindness and equality which the Quran ignores. It is for this reason that you will fight against tenderness in friendship if you follow Islam.

Let me finish my talk by giving you one more reason that Islam closes the door to tenderness and thereby to friendship.

Music and a tender heart

Islam commands that you should not benefit from music but act against it. Music is from God. Music is soft and tender and prepares tender hearts. The harmony between the voices and the sounds of instruments is to express feelings and emotions in beautiful and loving ways. Music in general strengthens friendship. Music is food to a grievous heart. But Islam fights against this tender means. Music is ordained in the Bible so that people can celebrate their salvation and their relationship with God.[8]

All the things you have heard in this message about Islam are dictatorial behaviors. Such behaviors are only to strengthen dictatorship which closes the door to peace, love and friendship. With Islam it will be difficult for you,

---

[8] Sing aloud to God our strength; shout for joy to the God of Jacob. Lift up a psalm, and bring the timbrel here, the pleasing lyre and harp. Blow the ram's horn in the new moon, in the time appointed, on our solemn feast day. For this *was* a Precept for Israel, an ordinance of the God of Jacob. (Psalm 81:1-4, MKJV)

if you desire to live in peace and harmony. You need Jesus and His Gospel.

Reflection Time 14

1. Why is it impossible to make genuine friends with anger, hatred, hostility, deception, lying and other dishonest means?
2. Why do we need to stay away from hating others?
3. Even though Islam is called a religion of peace by many, can this be supported with facts?
4. Isn't it good to invest our lives in love and kindness rather than in hatred and hostility?
5. Why do we need to follow Jesus Christ?

The Gospel of Jesus Christ Has Perfect Instructions for Relationships

These instructions are directed towards mind, heart and conscience. Together they confirm their superiority in comparison with other values. This is my goal in this presentation; to address the instructions of Jesus Christ to your mind, to your heart, to your conscience so that you can realize how unique, beneficial and life-changing they are.

Relationships are the most important parts of human life. If a belief does not create unity and harmony among people, it will be a total loss to spend life with that belief. Our beliefs shape our identities and attitudes in relationships. So, we need to choose which belief to follow or not to follow. It is therefore urgent for us to compare our belief with others' and see whether it is the best or we need to replace it with the best.

Love and kindness: The priorities of the Gospel in relationships

I mentioned that the instructions of the Gospel are perfect. This is because the Gospel believes that love and kindness are the key factors in building healthy relationships.

No other belief recognizes love and kindness as fundamental to relationships as does Jesus Christ.

All those beliefs that hold to evolutionary theory are unable doctrinally to say that there is a difference between kindness and cruelty. Why? Because, for them everything happens by accident. It is not therefore up to humankind to choose love and kindness as the surpassing factors in their relationships. These beliefs sacrifice the freedom of choice to the forces of nature and make people powerless. Investigating, evaluating and creative decision-making in relationship are therefore impossible. The reality is that they do not happen by accident, but by the words we speak and the attitudes we manifest.

In beliefs like New Age, Secular Humanism, Hinduism, Buddhism and others, each individual is taken as equal to God. Love and kindness become the vessels of self-centeredness and serve the individuals motives only.

Imagine in a family, love and kindness of a husband becomes irrelevant to his wife and the wife's to her husband or the children's to their parents since everybody is taught to be god and to follow his or her own model! A family or a society with such an individualistic ethic creates anarchy. It is not the individualistic model of a husband or a wife or a child or a leader that establishes a peaceful family or society. It is the values of the perfect model whose standard is above every other model.

In Islam also love and kindness are subject to the authority of the Muslim leader. It is therefore not love and kindness that rule in Islam, but the decision and power of the ruling authority. Consequently, no one in Islam, not even Muhammad, can be the perfect model of love and kindness since power and force make love and kindness conditional.

Jesus: The perfect model of love and kindness

Only Jesus can be the perfect model of love and kindness for you in your relationships with your family members and others. Why? Let me first raise couple of questions and then give you reasons for this.

What do you think the behaviors of a perfect model of love and kindness should be? What is the proper definition of this model?

This perfect model must be a person who practically demonstrates the excellence of love and kindness to all, friends and opponents. To friends, because true friendship is through love and kindness; to opponents, because they can pause a second and understand that opposition should not be to degrade but to present a better method in a peaceful way in order to restore peaceful relationships. No religion nor philosophy introduces such a model to the world, except the Gospel of Jesus Christ. This model is Jesus Christ Himself.

The Gospel of Jesus Christ says that God is love. If God were not love, His message and messenger also could not be loving. So, the first step in having loving relationships with others is to discover the true God who is the source of love and to build our life on His foundation. Our life needs to have a deeper connection with the source of love. That way we will never fall short of love and kindness in our relationships and never make excuses for hatred.

A true messenger and his belief must be based on love and kindness

Jesus Christ says in the Gospel (Matthew 22:37-40) that all the law and prophets must depend on two things: First, love God with all your heart, soul and mind. Second, love your neighbor as yourself. He is bringing forth the meaning that the true prophet and the true law must be based on love and kindness. If not, then neither the prophet nor his religion and law are from the loving God. Therefore, no matter how interested you are in having long-lasting peace or friendship with others, it will not happen by any model or prophet you follow unless you are following the perfect model of love and kindness in Jesus Christ.

If you follow an angry and dictatorial prophet or leader, his attitudes will be your standard towards your family and others. But if you follow Jesus, His unconditional love and kindness will be your standard towards others. There are huge differences between the words of the Quran and the Gospel concerning relationships. The Quran lacks the love and kindness which are for long-lasting friendship. Christ came to this world to teach us love and clean our hearts from hatred, cursing, hostility and war, but the last ten years of Muhammad's life was full of all of those things. Can there be a long lasting friendship with hatred, cursing, hostility and war? Absolutely not. Imagine if God hated and cursed you for your sin, and was always hostile to you. Would there be any hope for you to return to Him and become His friend? No. People become God's friend because of His love and compassion not because of His hostility. Abraham became the friend of God because God was friendly and kind not terrifying. This is true in our relationships too. People become friends with us if we are kind, loving and caring. Nobody becomes our sincere friend if we curse him or become hostile to him. That's why the Gospel in 1 John chapter 4 verses 11 and 12 says: Beloved, if God so loved us, we ought also to love one another.... If we love one another, God dwells in us, and His love is perfected in us. (MJKV)

The Gospel tells you to allow the God of love to live in you so that your love becomes perfect and then you can change even your enemies through that perfect love. Because any perfect thing draws attention, so does perfect love. With perfect love you may have a loving family, and you and your loving family will shine in your neighborhood and society. Your love also may amaze your opponents, and possibly they will follow your footsteps and become free of enmity. That's why you need to follow Jesus Christ and make His Gospel the crown of your head for your relationships in your family and with others.

Reflection Time 15

1. How would it be a problem if love and kindness are subjective, as in New Age, Islam and evolutionary worldviews, rather than objective, as in Jesus' teachings?
2. What do you think the characteristics of a perfect model of love and kindness should be?
3. What will our relational style be with people if we follow an angry and dictatorial leader or prophet?
4. Why do we need to discover the true God if we want to be established in love and kindness and have peace with others?
5. What kind of changes can love and kindness make in a family, in society and in the world?

6. Is it good to honor Jesus for His perfect love and kindness?

The Quran Asks the Prophet of Islam to Put His Trust in the Bible

Can you believe this? This is what I am going to talk about and amaze you.

There is much propaganda by strict Muslims that the Torah and the Gospel were changed. Is this true? In a previous topic, I touched on how the verses in the Quran say that the Quran was manipulated. Were the Torah and the Gospel also manipulated?

Muslims, who say that the Torah and the Gospel were altered haven't been able to build a logical case to prove whether this change happened during, before or after the time of Muhammad. Do you know why they haven't been able to build a logical argument for their claim? Because no matter what they say, it will also be against the words of the Quran.

The Torah and the Gospel could not have been altered before the time of Muhammad

Because Sura Yunus (10) in verse 94 says to Muhammad: If you Muhammad are in doubt as

210

to the Quran inquire of Christians and Jews who have read the Scriptures before you. Sura Al-e Imran (3) verse 3 and Sura Al Maeda (5) verses 46 to 48 also say that the Gospel and the Torah are a light and a guide to people.

We see that according to the Quran, Muhammad doubted in the authenticity of his own Quran but his god asked him to learn the truth from his contemporary Christians and Jews who were following the Gospel and the Torah. This shows that the Torah and the Gospel were not altered before Muhammad, otherwise his god would not call them the light of people and also would not ask Muhammad to learn the truth from Jews and Christians if they followed manipulated scriptures.

Neither could the alteration have happened in the time of Muhammad

Because Sura Al Baghara (2) in verses 91 and 97 and Sura An Nisa (4) in verse 47 say to Muhammad: The Quran is the confirmation of the Scriptures in the hands of Christians and Jews. Then Sura Al Maeda (5) in verse 68 says: O People of the Book! You have no ground to stand upon unless you stand fast by the Law, the

Gospel, and all the revelation that has come to you from your Lord ....

Wow! Not only does the Quran confirm the truthfulness of Muhammad's contemporary Torah and Gospel but it also instructs Jews and Christians to base their faith on them. The Quran would not confirm them if they were changed by Jews and Christians.

The alteration of the Torah and the Gospel could not have happened after the death of Muhammad

Because, as the Quran confirms, the true Torah and Gospel were everywhere in the whole of Arabian Peninsula and other surrounding areas that were occupied by the Islamic army. Muslim leaders and teachers from the first century of Islam would have kept the true Torah and Gospel which could have been used as proofs of any alteration. But there is no record in the ancient Islamic books and commentaries for this claim. This shows that the alteration claim has no basis.

The Quran Asks Muhammad to Lean on the Torah

I am amazed that Muslim leaders and clergies are not paying attention to two significant things in the Quran. Sura Yunus (10) in verses 94 and 95 asks Muhammad to lean on the Torah and Gospel. Sura Al Maeda (5) in verse 43 says that Jews must follow their own Torah and do not need to follow the Quran or Muhammad's decision.

Aren't you amazed that the god of the Quran asks Muhammad to put his trust in the Gospel and the Torah, but encourages Jews and Christians that they do not need to follow the Quran? In other words, there is a place for Muhammad and Muslims to doubt or deny the Quran but not the Torah according to the Quran. If Muhammad, as the supreme leader of Islam, is asked to lean on the Torah and the Gospel, then it becomes clear that Muslims, Muslim leaders, teachers and clergies also need to lean on Christian and Jewish Holy Scriptures, instead of spreading false accusations about them.

These verses of the Quran reflect Muhammad's high value of the Holy Scriptures in the hands of his contemporary Christians and Jews. Not only did he confirm the authority of these Holy books, he also encouraged Muslims to profess belief in them. Therefore, the Quran itself takes away every doubt of the Torah and the Gospel.

If Christians and Jews corrupted their scriptures and went astray, Muhammad would not want to rely on their Scriptures and customs. But we understand from the Islamic books that Muhammad attended a church in Mecca for years and was in contact with priests. His wife Khadijah always went to the church in Mecca. This was because of Muhammad's confidence in Christians. If these are the facts of Muhammad's life and he honored his contemporary Bible so much, where did this story of alteration originate?

This idea of accusation was begun after Muhammad fled from Mecca to Medina and took refuge in a Medinan tribe known as Khazraj who hated Jews and Christians. To survive and be accepted, Muhammad adjusted himself to the ways of that tribe. Hatred creates serious problems in peoples' relationships. If you start hating a person or a group of people, that hatred leads you to create many false accusations against them, even call them the worst of beasts and wish death on them.

This was what happened with Muhammad in Medina. While he was in Mecca he treated Jews and Christians as good role models, and called their Scriptures a light for people. But after fleeing to Medina, he called them the worst of beasts, ignored the significance of their Scriptures and furthermore forced them to leave their religions and become Muslims. What he did to Jews and Christians afterwards was completely the opposite of the instructions the Quran gives in the first era of Muhammad's ministry in Mecca. His logic was that his god had changed his mind about Jews, Christians and their Scriptures in order to please Muhammad. Does the true God speak against His own words and instructions at the cost of the truth? Not at all. This is one of the reasons that caused me to lose confidence in the Quran.

As Muhammad's power was increasing in Medina year after year, the Quran was getting far from its original doctrine. It was becoming more confusing to people, even to his own people as some became angry and left Islam for new-found unfairness and hostility to people. The

Muhammad of Medina was not the Muhammad of Mecca anymore. In Mecca, he was a peaceful man and did not push pagans to follow him. Jews and Christians were on the right path for following the Bible. He was even attending a church with his wife Khadijah. But in Medina he became pushy and cherished hatred towards Jews and Christians, using excuses that his god changed his mind to please him.

In Medina, he was under pressure to search for any excuse to blame Jews and Christians in order to please his hosting tribe. He even taught his followers that his name was foretold in the Torah and the Gospel (Suras 7:157 and 61:6), so that his followers could in the future blame the Jews and Christians of forging the Bible if they could not find his name there. Years after Muhammad's death, Muslim teachers discovered that Muhammad's name did not exist in the Bible. Since it was illegal for them to shed any doubt on Muhammad's and the Quran's words, the easier and safer option was for them to blame Christians and Jews of corrupting the Bible and removing the name of Muhammad. Therefore, the news of the "removal of the name of Muhammad from the Bible" became wide-spread amongst Muslims.

So we can see how Muhammad changed his attitudes towards Jews and Christians after his migration to Medina. This opened the door for his successors to denounce the Bible with a baseless accusation and lead Muslims worldwide to blame Jews and Christians.

The fear of speaking the truth has now blocked the way for Muslim leaders and teachers to approach the existing disunity between the Quran and the Bible in a logical and theological way.

For Muslim leaders and teachers, the validity of the Bible is surprisingly not based on its message but rather on whether it contains the name of Muhammad or not. The real differences between these two books is not the existence or absence of a name; it is the salvation which the Bible provides for its followers in the life on earth that the Quran does not.

Suppose Muhammad's name was in the Bible. What difference would it make? Nothing. The central message of the Bible is that you need to put your trust in Jesus Christ, who is alive, in heaven and able to lead you to heaven. If Muhammad's name was in the Bible, it would still ask you to put your trust in Jesus. Why? Because, only Jesus is the way, the truth and the life that lead to heaven.

The message of the Bible from Adam to Jesus is summarized in the fact that peoples' salvation is the most important thing to God. For this reason, God revealed Himself personally in Jesus Christ in order to save people from the bondage of sin and Satan. So the major concern of God in the Bible is not the absence or existence of a prophet's name, but the salvation of people, which is more important than anyone's name.

The entire Bible of Jesus Christ came into its fullness as a book by 40 prophets over 1600 years. With more than 300 prophesies, they all looked to the day when Jesus Christ would come and save the world. Neither the political instability nor the economic and social fluctuations were able to create any disharmony among the messages of these 40 prophets of the Bible over such a long period of time. These prophesies were all fulfilled with the coming of Jesus Christ. But disharmony is rampant in the Quran, even though it is by one man alone, Muhammad, within the short time of 23 years of his mission. Despite this short time, many verses of the Quran from the last 10 years of Muhammad's life are opposite to the early Meccan verses. Aren't you amazed at the harmony of the messages of the many prophets in the Bible in the 1600 year time frame?

My curiosity led me to read and test the words of the Bible of Jesus Christ personally because of the Muslim leaders' rejection of it. I said to myself, God has given me eyes to see and read, a brain to compare, a heart and conscience to evaluate and decide. This opened the door for me to find that the Bible of Christ puts the hands of man in the hands of God. The Quran never does this. For this reason I gave my heart to Jesus.

You need to do the same and take personal initiatives to see whether the Quran or the Bible of Jesus Christ is genuine, and choose the one that gives you the assurance of salvation. Neither the Quran nor Muhammad are able to give you assurance of salvation. Sura Lughman (31) verse 34 and Sura Al Ahghaf (46) verse 9 say that no one knows what will happen to him after death. But the Bible says those who follow Christ are already saved and will directly go to the arms of God after they die. Therefore, put your trust in the Bible of Jesus Christ and be saved.

Reflection Time 16

1. Would Muhammad have put his trust in the Bible if he thought it was manipulated?

2. Can any factual case be made for the accusations that Muslim scholars make concerning the so-called changes made to the Bible?

3. One reason for Muslim scholars' accusation is the absence of Muhammad's name in the Bible. Would it make any difference in the central message of the Bible if his name was in the Bible?

4. What do we need to do to draw Muslims' attention more toward their own salvation (since it is God's major concern) and be less worried about the absence or existence of a name in the Bible?

5. Which book do we need to follow - the Bible that provides assurance of salvation or the Quran that lacks it?

Islam's Accusations of Christians' Beliefs Are Baseless

Islam blames Christians for things which they never believed. One example is the misinterpretation of the phrase "Son of God". The followers of Jesus believe in a spiritual way that Jesus is the Son of God and they themselves are the children[9] of God.

To call Jesus "the Son of God" is slanderous in Islam

The Quran in Sura An-Nisa (4) verse 171 says that it is far from God to have a son. And in Sura Maryam verses 35, 89 and 91 says that it is evil, disastrous and monstrous to mention a son for God. Based on these statements of the Quran and contrary to its true meaning in the Gospel of Jesus Christ, Islamic commentaries interpret the

---

[9] The Gospel says, "Blessed *are* the peacemakers: for they shall be called the children of God." (Matthew 5:9) Jesus is called the Son of God because not only is He the peacemaker but also the Prince of Peace. His followers are also called the children of God because they are established in peace by Jesus to be His ambassadors for peace.

phrase "Son of God" falsely and call it "the slanders of Christians against God". They say that Christians hold the belief that Jesus came to this world as the result of a physical relationship between God and Mary.

Nowhere in the Christian Bible is it stated that Jesus was born as the result of a physical relationship between God and Mary. Instead, it says that with the coming of the Spirit of God upon the Virgin Mary, the Spirit became flesh and revealed Himself fully in Jesus Christ. The relationship of God and Mary in the Gospel is a spiritual relationship. God does not need a wife and cannot have a worldly relationship with a woman because He is God.

Neglecting the truth about the phrase "Son of God"

Isn't this shocking? Muhammad and Muslim scholars closed their eyes to the true meaning of this phrase in the Gospel, but called Christians insulting and sanctioned Muslims to kill Christians for their own misinterpretation and misunderstanding. That's why every Muslim needs to borrow a Gospel from a Christian, read it and understand personally that Islam's accusations of Christians' beliefs are untrue. Muslims need to know what it means to be called the son or daughter of God and put an end to the 1400 years of Islamic misunderstanding, prejudice and harsh reaction to Christians' and Jewish beliefs.

The Gospel states the conception of Jesus in Mary from the book of Luke chapter 1 verse 35 in this way: "And the angel answered and said to Mary, The Holy Spirit shall come on you, and the power of the Highest shall overshadow you. Therefore, also that Holy One which will be born of you shall be called Son of God." (MKJV) You see that the Gospel is clearly saying that the Spirit of God came upon Mary and she became pregnant with the holy child Jesus. This was therefore a spiritual relationship not a physical relationship.

Concerning the followers of Jesus Christ also, the Gospel in the book of John chapter 1 verses 12 and 13 says that Jesus gave the right to those who believed in Him to be called the children of God. They are children born not of man's will nor of flesh and blood, but of God SPIRITUALLY because of their faith in Jesus Christ. The Gospel again in the book of 1st Peter chapter 1 verse 23 says to the followers of Jesus Christ: "having been born again, not of corruptible seed, but of incorruptible, through the living Word of God, and abiding forever." (MKJV)

So, Jesus is called the Son of God because He is the living and eternal Spirit and Word of God; we are called the children of God because Jesus lives in us as the eternal Spirit and Word of God, and has given us eternal life and assurance. Therefore, the interpretations of Islamic books and commentaries in regard to Christians' belief about the Son of God is absolutely wrong. Muslim scholars need to read the Gospel and stop blaming Christians baselessly.

The Quran says that Allah can have a son

Now I want to show you couple of interesting things from the Quran. The Sura Maryam (19) in verses 89 and 91 says that to invoke a son for God is a terrible evil thing. But Sura Az-Zumar (39) in verse 4 says that God can have a son if He desires. If invoking a son for God is evil why does the Quran itself open a door for people to invoke a son to God?

Aren't Muslim scholars able to see this problem in the Quran? They call Christians slanderous for believing that God can have a son. Isn't therefore Sura Az Zumar slanderous for saying that God can have a son if He desires? On one hand the Quran in Sura An-Nisa (4) verse 171 says that God can never have a son, but on the other hand Sura Az-Zumar (39) in verse 4 says that God can have a son if He desires. Did you get it? Sura Az-Zumar is saying that it is not impossible for God to have a son.

Isn't this hypocrisy? On one hand, the Quran says to Christians that God cannot have a son, but on the other hand says to Muslims, yes, if God desires He can have a son. This is therefore unjust when the Quran itself confirms that God can have a son, but aims to deprive Jews and Christians of this belief. It further instructs Muslims to kill them for having such a belief. It is very unjust.

Sura Al Tawba (9) in verses 29 and 30 says: Make war upon such of those to whom the Scriptures have been given .... The Jews say, 'Ezra or Ozair is a son of God'; and the Christians say, 'The Messiah is a son of God.' ....

There is a way to stay away from baseless accusations

I hope you noticed why the Quran does not have any legitimate right to accuse Jews and Christians and fight against them for believing that God can have a son. First, because Christians believe it in a spiritual way, second, the Quran itself says in Sura Az-Zumar that God can have a son. Muslim scholars should therefore be ashamed of themselves for blaming Christians and Jews and for spreading false accusations against them everywhere. They need to apologize to Jews and Christians. The entire interpretation of Islamic books and commentaries in regard to Christians' belief about the Son of God is absolutely wrong. Muslim writers will not be able to reflect a true view of Christianity unless they read the Gospel. They need to leave the traditional restrictions of Islam behind and read the Gospel and the commentaries over the words of the Gospel in order to be able to understand Christians' approach to the Son-hood of Jesus Christ.

I was the same when I was a Muslim. There was always cultural pressure on people like me to follow traditions, no matter if they were right or wrong. But I am so grateful that in one stage of my life my mind and heart desired to look at life outside of Islam. It was then that Jesus revealed Himself to me and changed my world view.

Unlike Christian belief, Islam interprets the Trinity as three gods

I want to share with you another one of Islam's baseless accusation against Christians regarding the Trinity.

The Quran (An-Nisa 4:171; Al Maeda 5: 116) and the Islamic commentaries say that Christians believe in three gods. This is absolutely untrue. It is blasphemy in the Bible of Jesus Christ to believe in more than One God. The Gospel says numerous times that "God is One" (Mark 12:32; Romans 3:30; 1 Corinthians 8: 4; Galatians 3:20; 1 Timothy 2:5).

There is no support for three gods in the Gospel at all. Islam has distorted the Truth in order to have an excuse to condemn Christians. Christians never interpret the Trinity in the Gospel to mean three gods. All interpretation and commentaries lead to belief in the One true God.

What is the Trinity in Christian belief? It is the Father, the Son and the Holy Spirit. As the loving and forgiving God, Christians call Him the Spiritual Father. As the establisher of His Spiritual Kingdom in our hearts on earth, He is called the Son. And as the protecting, assuring and guiding God on earth, He is called the Holy Spirit. So the meaning of the Trinity is that the same God reveals Himself in three ways to us.

We as individuals also have the similar kind of titles in our lives on earth. I am called a son, a husband, a father. Though I am one person, I reveal myself in three ways or as three persons in order to express my love and responsibility in my family. This does not mean that I am three independent persons. I am one person but manifesting myself as three. This is the same with God.

God Himself never needs these names; they are all for the benefit of humanity. Humanity needs pure love which is in God only. Since in our daily lives, no love surpasses the love of parents toward their children, God calls Himself the Father, proving that He loves us with a parental heart even more than our parents.

See how God describes His love and care in the Bible

In the book of the prophet Isaiah chapter 66 verse 13 He says: "As one whom his mother comforts, so I will comfort you; ...." (NKJV) Again in the book of Isaiah chapter 49 verse 15 God says: "Can a woman forget her suckling child, that she should not have compassion on the son of her womb? Yes, they may forget, yet I will not forget you." (MKJV) Jesus says in the book of Matthew chapter 7 verse 11 in the Gospel: "If you then, being evil, know how to give good gifts to your children, how much more shall your Father in Heaven give good things to those who ask Him?" (MKJV)

So God's love is a parental love for us. He approaches us with an intimate and fatherly love to teach us what true love, justice, holiness, righteousness, peace and joy are. For these reasons, He is called the Father.

God is also called the Son

The Spirit of God came upon Mary and the Spirit was born of the flesh as Jesus. This means God revealed Himself in Jesus. God is able and He can reveal Himself in any way He desires. He revealed Himself as a fire to Moses and as a man in Jesus for us.

Why does God want to reveal Himself? Why doesn't He hide himself like the god of Islam? Because He has a heavenly plan to implement on earth. The heavenly plan can be engineered on earth by God only since no one else knows the plan well as God does.

God is also called the Spirit

Also, God has created humanity for a purpose. To give purpose to life, God's constant presence and supervision are necessary. He is the architect to establish his Kingdom in our hearts. An architect does two things: First, he writes everything on paper, second, he goes to the sight for building. God does the same. He prepared the Bible as His written Word on how to establish His spiritual kingdom in our hearts. He then revealed Himself in Jesus and walked into our lives to establish His kingdom in our hearts as well.

How can the words of God be relevant to us if we do not have the person of God with us? That's why the Gospel says in the book of John chapter 1 verse 14: "The Word was made flesh, and dwelt among us, and we beheld his glory, the glory as of the only begotten of the Father, full of grace and truth." (KJV) So God revealed Himself in Jesus and called His person in this revelation "the Son" in order to build His spiritual kingdom on earth.

Also as the omnipresent, teaching, comforting, protecting, assuring and guiding God, He is called the Holy Spirit in the Gospel. For God to be the only loving God and Savior is not enough for humanity. We also need His continual presence to remind us and to protect us, like a mother or father to hold our hands to the end of our journey in this world. This continual presence of God with us on earth is called the Holy Spirit in the Gospel. So the Trinity does not mean three gods, but the manifestation of One God in three ways. Therefore the Muslim scholars' accusations of Christians are baseless.

I will finish my talk with one more shocking and unbelievable accusation of the Quran. It says in Sura Al Tawba (9) verse 31: "Jews and Christians take their teachers and their monks as lords beside God, ..."

There is no such teaching in the entire Bible nor in Jewish nor Christian history. It is utterly a baseless accusation. The Gospel and Christians believe in One God only. Islam's accusations of Christians' beliefs are baseless.

Reflection Time 17

1. The Gospel (Luke chapter 1 verse 35) and the Quran (Sura Maryam verses 17 to 21) both say that God sent His Spirit to the Virgin Mary and she gave birth to a holy Son. Why would Muslim scholars then ignore this obvious spiritual relationship between God and Mary, and falsely attribute to Christianity that Jesus was the result of a physical relationship between God and Mary?

2. How sincere could Muslim Scholars be in their objection to calling Jesus "the Son of God" since the Quran itself confirms that God can have a son if he wishes?

3. It is blasphemy to believe in more than One God in the Bible. Christians have never interpreted the Trinity as three gods, why then would Muhammad and Muslim scholars claim that Christians believe in three gods?

4. What can help Muslims free themselves of misinformation and false accusations?

5. As a Muslim, Daniel also accused Christians about the Trinity and Sonhood of Jesus Christ. How did his views change?

The Political Game in Islam Disregards Its Own Beliefs

Doctrinally, Islam is the only political religion in the world. Generally speaking, politics is not immune from lies and deception. Not only has Islamic politics not stayed away from lies and deception, but has gone even further and made them legitimate in some circumstances.

Suras Al-e Imran (3) verse 54 and Al Anfal (8) verse 30 say: Allah is the best of deceivers. If Allah is the best of deceivers, this means that he will use his deception in everything, including politics. If Allah uses deception in politics, don't you think that his faithful servants will follow in his footsteps? There is no doubt that they will follow his politics.

The legitimacy of deception in Islam has cost Muslims a great deal since the rise of Islam up until now. Deception opened the door to lying and political games, even within the Islamic community.

The Quran also says that Allah Legitimized Lying. Sura An Nahl (16) verse 106 teaches that there are circumstances that can "compel" a Muslim to tell a lie. Sura Al Baghara (2) verse 225 encourages Muslims to deny their faith in Allah if the condition necessitates until the situation gets back to normal. Sura Al-e Imran (3) verse 28 tells Muslims to be friends with non-Muslims until Muslims get to power and rule or do something against them.

You see that the god of Islam encourages his followers to lie and live with dishonesty among others.

As a result, lying influenced Islamic relationships and the judiciary system. The famous Hadith writer Bukhari writes in his hadith number 857 of the Book 49 in Volume 3 that Muhammed the prophet of Islam said: A man who brings peace to the people by making up good words or by saying nice things, though untrue, does not lie.

Imagine what happens when the god and prophet of a nation give license for lying! It is for this reason that Taghiyya or convenient lying hasn't allowed sincerity to grow among Muslim nations.

According to the Bible, only truth, not a lie, can create sincere and peaceful relationships. Lying and deception were legitimized by Allah,

Muhammad and Muslim scholars and became a part of Islamic faith and politics. What Happened Then? Deception and lying made political games unavoidable in Islamic politics and caused Islamic beliefs to be unstable.

Because of political games, Muhammad himself changed the principles of Islam.

Seeing that the prophet of Islam changed the principles of Islam continually and without hesitation, his successors thus imitated him to the point of even disregarding Muhammad's commands and traditions after his death. These changes to the Islamic beliefs were imposed on Islamic people.

The Bible rejects any kind of deception and lying. In the book of Solomon's Proverbs chapter 14 verses 5 and 25 the Bible says: "A truthful witness doesn't deceive, but a false witness pours out lies. ... a truthful witness saves lives, but a false witness is deceitful." (NIV) The Gospel also says in 2 Corinthians chapter 4 verse 2: "We have renounced the hidden things of dishonesty, not walking in craftiness, nor handling the word of God deceitfully; but by manifestation of the truth commending ourselves to every man's conscience in the sight of God." (NIV) The Bible clearly rejects deceit and lies. However, the Quran makes them an essential part of Islamic belief, leading to political games and chaos.

The first example of political games in Islam is the changing of the direction in which Muslims pray

For about fifteen years Muhammad's direction for prayer, or Ghiblah, was Jerusalem and he and his followers prayed five times a day towards that city. This was a time when he was still hoping to draw Jews to his Islam and accept him as their prophet. But they rejected him since prophets had to come from the line of Isaac. Because of this, Muhammad disliked the Jews and did not want to pray towards the Jewish city of Jerusalem. He changed his prayer direction therefore from the One God sanctuary in Jerusalem to the Ka'ba where hundreds of idols were still being worshipped by pagans. Sura Al Baghara (2) in verses 142 and 145 tells us that Allah confirmed the change of the Ghiblah to please Muhammad. As a result, a significant belief of Islam was sacrificed to political games.

The changing of Ghiblah in Islam is nothing but an indication of the instability of Islamic doctrine. The true God would not ask his prophet to turn his face from the One-God sanctuary to a temple of idols.

The second problem is what Sura Al Baghara (2) says that Allah confirmed the change of the Ghiblah to please Muhammad. Whereas in a true belief, it is the prophet and the people that should please the sinless God, not God to please the motives of a sinful man. This saying in the Quran is not logical.

What Muhammad did was a political game. Since he had lost his hope about Jews becoming Muslims, he decided to invest in pagans and draw their attention to Islam. For this reason, he gave up Jerusalem and chose Ka'ba as the Ghiblah for himself and all Muslims.

The second example of political games in Islam is to penetrate by peace, then rule by force

In the first 13 years of his preaching, Muhammad said: "Let there be no compulsion in religion", which is now 256th verse of the Sura Al Baghara

(2) of the Quran. At the time, he only had 150 followers. In the last 10 years of his life when he had many more followers, Muhammad put himself in the position of the unquestionable political and religious leader, and therefore forced all people groups in the Arabian Peninsula to become his followers. Then the language of the Quran changed from stating "there should be no-compulsion in religion" to "no religion other than Islam shall be accepted" which is stated in Sura Al-e Imran (3) verse 85.

This political game in Islam became the standard of many Muslim leaders after Muhammad, which has acted like a poison to trust and intimacy. As we go forward, you will see the negative effects of it on every aspect of life.

The third example of political games in Islam is the use of manipulation for power

The constant changes brought about by Muhammad in his approach toward others meant to his successors that a Muslim leader has the authority to do everything he wants. Muslim leaders who came to power after Muhammad, Abu Baker, Omar, Othman and Ali had inherited the political instability from Muhammad and learned that they could change everything in Islam based on convenience.

His son-in-law Ali claimed to be the only legitimate leader, but the father-in-laws and the brother-in-law preferred leadership by seniority. The tension among them led to the creation of Sunni and Shia sects, which brought on countless killings.

The fourth example of political games in Islam is the change of the location of the Ka'ba

Did you know that the political games and tension in Islam caused the change of the Ka'ba in Becca or Mecca from Petra in Jordan to the present Mecca in Saudi Arabia? This happened in the year 64 After Hijra or the year 683 After Christ. The Ka'ba of Petra was the place of pilgrimage for hajj for Muhammad, Abu Baker, Omar, Othman and Ali. They were all born and raised in Petra. They had never been in the present Mecca for pilgrimage. All Qurayshis (Ghorayshis) and Hashemites lived in Petra. No wonder the present kingdom in Jordan calls itself the Hashemite. Muhammad was a Hashemite. It was in Petra that he claimed to be a prophet. The Ka'ba in Petra was ruined in the time of Yazid ibn Muaviyah and the new Ka'ba was built in Saudi Arabia.

The Jordanian people strongly hold to the claim that they are the only Hashemites. The kingdom of Jordan has placed a huge flag at the border of Jordan and Saudi Arabia. The only word on this flag is Hashemite, which means we Jordanians are the only Hashemites not you Saudi Arabians.

Let me first give you references from the Quran and then from the Islamic and non-Islamic historical books on why the present Mecca cannot be the original Mecca of Muhammad. Then I will tell you why the Ka'ba was closed down in Jordan but established in Saudi Arabia.

The present Mecca does not match the Mecca mentioned in the Quran

The verses of the Quran about the Ka'ba match the description of Petra instead of the present Mecca. Sura Al-e Imran (3) in verses 96 and 97 says that the sanctuary that Abraham built was in Becca. Sura Al Fath (48) verse 24 is speaking about the army of Islam that conquered the Ka'ba which was in the valley of Mecca. Only the Ka'ba in Petra was in the valley but there is no valley near the present Ka'ba or in its surrounding areas.

Also, *the present Mecca does not match the historical evidence*

You know that the pre-Islamic pagans also practiced the ceremony of Hajj. Early writings about the Ka'ba say that it was built in a valley. Historians and archeologists refer to many cities in Saudi Arabia with different pagan shrines before and in the time of Muhammad, but not to a city in the southern part of Saudi Arabia by the name of Mecca. How could a very important and large religious city which was also on a significant trading route, be hidden from the eyes of historians and archeologists? They did not write about it, because it did not exist in Saudi Arabia. It existed in Jordan. All historical evidence shows that the major pre-Islamic pilgrimages for Hajj were always made to Petra, which had the black-stone or Hajar-ol Asvad and the Ka'ba or Beytol-Haram.

The Black Stone played a major role in drawing pilgrims to Petra. 400 years before Muhammad, the Greek philosopher Maximus of Tyre said that the Black Stone was in Petra. The Greek

Encyclopedia Suda (Souda) also mentions the fact that the Black Stone was in Petra.

Tabari, the famous ancient Islamic historian, says on pages 192 to 198 of his history book that Abraham and Ishmael built the Ka'ba in a valley. On pages 712 to 713, Tabari speaks again about the childhood of Muhammad, playing with boys in a valley in the holy city. There was also a small stream next to the Ka'ba.

There are references to farm lands, fruit trees and vineyards near Ka'ba in the old writings, whereas it is hard to attribute any fertile land to the present dry land of Mecca. Near the present Ka'ba there is neither valley nor stream nor farm lands nor fruit trees.

History gives us more information that the holy city was surrounded by walls and mountains. The entry to the city was through two cracks or Thaniyas in the rocks of the mountains. Muhammad entered the city through these cracks.

The present city of Mecca does not have any signs of ancient walls, mountains or rocks surrounding it and no entry through the cracks of rocks. But all these descriptions match the present Petra in Jordan.

The two mountains of Safa and Marwah are significant in Islamic Hajj. In ancient historical writings they are two huge mountains in Petra that had idols and shrines at the top. People climbed the mountains up many steps in order to worship the idols. In the present Mecca there are only two very small man-made mounds that are called Safa and Marwa and are inside a mosque.

Mount Hira had a cave where Muhammad spent a lot of time fasting and praying as a pagan before claiming to be a Muslim prophet. In Islamic literature, Mount Hira faced the city and was located in the upper part of Mecca. But today's Mount Hira is far from the Ka'ba and does not face the city.

Petra is to the north of Medina and the present Mecca is to the south. But the historical books are saying to us that Qurayshi armies always attacked Medina from the north. Also, during the Battle of the Ditch, Medina was protected by a Ditch between two mountains on the north side of the city.

Muslim armies marching out of Medina to attack Mecca always marched north from Medina towards Petra rather than to the south toward the present Mecca. In other words, the actual holy city or Mecca was north of Medina not south.

Early mosques also point to Petra. All mosques should face Ka'ba according to Islamic tradition. The mosques that were built from the time of Muhammad until the year 107 After Hijra or the year 725 After Christ all faced Petra. During the next hundred years new mosques began to point in different directions because of tensions among Muslim groups over the two Ka'bas. In the year 133 After Hijra or the year 750 After Christ the Abbasid government in Iraq captured Syria and made Baghdad the center of Islamic rule. From this point on the Middle Eastern mosques started to pray towards the new Ka'ba in Saudi Arabia.

How did this change from Petra to Mecca happen?

Three decades after the death of Muhammad which is the year 64 After Hijra or the year 683 After Christ, Abdullah ibn az- Zubayr the governor of Petra rebelled against caliph Yazid of the Umayyad Dynasty in Damascus of Syria and announced himself the caliph. Tabari tells us that Abdullah demolished the Ka'ba and leveled it to the ground, took the Black Stone and moved to a remote area in the present Mecca. He did this in order to distance himself from the revenge of Umayyads, and also to build a new Ka'ba and place the Black Stone there for pilgrims' attention to the new Ka'ba. He knew the heart of Muslims had to be wherever the Black Stone was.

Three Umayyad rulers died during this time, one after the other, causing internal problems for the Umayyad government to fight Abdullah for the return of the Black Stone to Petra. The weakness of the Umayyad government caused Abdullah to succeed in his endeavor to establish a new Ka'ba, as well as a pilgrimage center and prayer direction for Muslims.

In the year 68 After Hijra or the year 687 after Christ, there were different pilgrimages to different locations. Some went to Petra hoping that the Black Stone would be returned. Some others went to the present Mecca, because the Black Stone was there. In the year 71 After Hijra or the year 689 After Christ, the city of Kufa in Iraq rebelled against the Umayyads and joined Abdullah in promoting the new Ka'ba. In the year

94 After Hijra or the year 713 After Christ an earthquake destroyed much of Petra and the city was abandoned. Many interpreted it as Allah's denunciation of Petra and acceptance of the new Ka'ba. Then in the year 128 After Hijra or the year 745 After Christ another earthquake destroyed buildings in Syria and Jordan. As a result all hope of returning the Black Stone to Petra was lost. In the year 133 After Hijra or the year 750 After Christ the Abbasids of Iraq overthrew the Umayyads in Syria and most Muslims in the M. East began to pray towards the new Ka'ba in Saudi Arabia.

But there were still opponents to the new Ka'ba and Mecca. Qarmatians, who rebelled against the Abbasids and took control of Bahrain, were strictly against any pilgrimage to the new Ka'ba and killed many Muslim pilgrims going there. In the year 930 After Christ, they invaded the present Mecca and removed the Black Stone and kept it for 21 years and did not give it back to the Abbasids. The removal of the Black Stone created catastrophe for the pilgrimage. Eventually, the Abbasids in Iraq paid a huge amount of money to the Qarmatians to get the Black Stone back. The

Black Stone was not a piece anymore but was broken into several pieces by the Qarmatians.

Do you see how did political games and tensions changed even the most sacred center of Islam from Petra to the present Mecca? Do you realize that Islam does not have a solid standard, every leader does whatever he likes? How can this unstable politics be beneficial for you? It cannot be.

I want to tell you one more political game from Islam and then finish.

The fifth example of Islamic political games is that the land of Israel belongs to Palestinians not the Jews

Sura Al Maeda (5) in verses 21 and 22 says that Allah ordained Israel for Jews and it belongs to them forever but not to Palestinians or any other groups. Sura Al Isra (17) verse 104 says to the children of Israel to dwell in the Holy Land and when the time of promise arrives, God will also bring many scattered Jews from various countries to Israel.

Against the teachings of the Quran, you were taught that Jews have occupied Israel. Some Islamic governments and leaders have been sending millions of dollars every year to Palestinians, Hezbollah and other groups to drive Jews out of Israel, the Land which the Quran says God has given to the Jews forever.

Isn't it heart breaking that so much money is wasted on a lie, when it could be used for millions of needy people in Islamic countries? Isn't it heartbreaking that many young people are stirred to get involved in terrorism against Jews just because of lies and political games? Muslim leaders have been keeping Muslims in the dark with their lies and political games. This has cost Muslim nations a great deal. You can only overcome these deceptions, lies and political games by being awakened. Only through Jesus Christ can we overcome these political games.

Reflection Time 18

1. In what ways does the belief that Allah is the best of deceivers affect his religion and the lives of his followers?
2. Lying and deception are legitimized in Islam under some circumstances; this is called

Taqiyya or Convenient Lying or deception. Doesn't this mean that people are taught by Allah and his religion to lie and deceive?

3. Lying and deception in Islam opened a door to political games. Give an example of how this political game blocked the way to a sincere and peaceful relationship among Muslims?

4. Give some examples of how legitimizing lying and deceit ended up making Islam's own doctrine vulnerable to constant changes.

5. Do people need to base their lives on a belief that rejects all deception and lying and teaches them only moral values? Why?

6. What will happen if Muslims remain unaware of the best values?

7. Do we have a responsibility to create awareness of the best values among Muslims?

The Comfort of Becoming Free from Bluffs, Lies and Political Games.

It really hurts when someone deceives you or hides the truth from you. As much as the lying and deception of others can hurt you, your lying and deception also can hurt others. They hurt everyone. The solution is that you need to stay away from them before expecting others to stay away from them.

It will also be very comforting for you and your family to become free from all kinds of lying, deception and political games and to establish your life on truth and honesty. It will give everyone a sense of security. For this you need to follow a belief that not only does not promote lying, deception and bluffing but also cuts to the root of them in your heart through knowledge and makes you free.

In my previous talk I mentioned how pretending, lying, deceiving and political games have their roots in Islam and how they have been costing Muslim nations a great deal since the rise of Islam.

The way to protect yourself from political game

How can you protect yourself from such unethical things that are part of Islamic politics? You cannot, because Islam allows them to penetrate into every sphere of life. The Quran states that Allah is the best of deceivers. This gives way to Muslims to justify their own deception and lying and think that they are ok since Allah himself uses them.

Have you ever thought that lying, deceiving, bluffing or any other unethical game are roadblocks to peace and comfort everywhere and in your own family too? No matter whom you deceive, you will more likely cause that person to react with similar excuses or motives. Both of you will lose trust in one another. Of course, no trust means no peace nor comfort. That's why peace, comfort and real love are lacking in many families, because deception and lies have destroyed trust. Members of these families learn how to deceive and how to live with deception. Husbands and wives, parents and children have learned how and where to cleverly lie and deceive. Very sad, isn't it?

I have never forgotten a comment from a professor of law in the university where I was studying for my bachelor's degree in my motherland. He was critical and saying, "I wonder why bribing is not legal since everybody practices it." He also said, "Why don't we reveal our most practiced daily ethic to others and tell them openly that not a single day in our life goes forward without lies and deception"

This is the reality in all Islamic countries. Life in all of them is affected by the Islamic unethical codes of conduct and many people do not mind using lies and deception in their relationships. As someone put it: "We call each other brothers first and then deceive one another."

Courage to overcome the dark values and become free

I sincerely admire the courage of men and women who see the dark spots in their own society and culture, have the courage to reveal it and cry out for a remedy to break these chains. Such people are more likely to leave Islam and find a better path for themselves.

Wouldn't it be encouraging to become free from such an unpleasant life and walk in light like the light of a lamp on a hill that everybody can benefit from? Everybody - you, your family and others. It is also immeasurably more comforting and peaceful to become a model of light for your own family instead of a model of darkness that promotes lies and deception. That moment will become an amazing moment when your life is changed and you are able to say, "Ah, I am free now. My yes is a real yes now, my no is a real no too. I don't need to twist my words anymore. Because the light is my model now, not darkness." This is what a true belief does for you. Not only does it not teach you deception and lying, but cuts to the root of them in your heart and makes you a heavenly being, a heavenly prince and princess. Yes, a heavenly being. You will then be able to walk with the true God, shine as His agent amongst people and become a light for them.

Islam is a barrier to freedom from bluffs, lying, deception and political games

I am 100% sure that Islam is a barrier for you to walk with God. That's why I left Islam and became a follower of Jesus Christ. I wanted to have peace in my own family and in my relationships with others, but Islam was a barrier with its Taqiyah or convenient lying and deception. There was a moment in my life when I realized that I did not want to practice Islam anymore. I did not dare to reveal this to my wife, extended family members, friends nor others, because of Islamic punishment. Islam deals with you like a chained person. Islam does not believe in freedom and does not allow you to leave it. You have only two choices, confess and die or lie and live. Since it is very popular to lie and live, you also become like most of the leaders and people, lie and live. But fortune knocked on my door when I realized that I needed to find a way to get myself unchained from Islam which had torn peace and comfort from me. I was thirsting for peace and comfort within. So that thirst in me led me to overcome Islamic pressures in my heart in order to have peace and comfort.

You can be free if you want

You know, if you have the world but do not have peace and comfort in your heart, you feel that you have nothing. It is then that you stand to do something and bring peace into your life. We have an idiom in the Iranian language which says: "You can if you want." In other words, if you desire a thing and take a step toward it, you may have it. I took steps toward peace and comfort, but they actually rushed toward me. If you get out of your messy life and take one step toward peace, Jesus the Prince of Peace takes one hundred steps toward you. This was what happened to me. I desperately needed to allow Jesus Christ and His Gospel to become the light of my life. The Gospel says in the book of 1 John chapter 2 verse 21 that no lie comes from the truth. (NIV) When I read that, I realized that Islam cannot be of the truth since it legitimizes lying and deception. Those are not from the truth and are enemies of peaceful relationships.

The Prophet Solomon says in his book Proverbs chapter 12 verse 22: The Lord detests lying lips, but he delights in men who are truthful. (NIV) The true God hates bluffs, lies and political games. Why? Because they destroy peace and comfort between you and God, and between you and others.

Do you desire God to be happy with you and take delight in you?

Not only did I want to have peace in my own heart, in my own family and in my relationships with others, but I also wanted to have peace with my God. Then He could be happy with me and take delight in me as the Prophet Solomon had said.

None of these could happen to me if I remained a Muslim. But all of them became parts of my life after I gave my heart to Jesus. The light of Jesus Christ unveiled and uprooted the destructive things in me, and led me to the source of absolute love, holiness, peace and comfort.

The change in my life also amazed my wife and encouraged her to read the Gospel of Jesus Christ. As a result, she also gave her heart to Jesus. She discovered that it was impossible to have a peaceful marital relationship with the presence of Islam and without the presence of Jesus. By reading the Gospel many other things were also revealed to her. For example, she discovered that Jesus said a man should have one wife only, husbands and wives should love each other like their own bodies. She said, "this is fantastic, one wife and one husband." She loved it. Everything became clear to her. She realized that husbands and wives, governments and people can never have peace with each other if they follow a belief that promotes lies and deception. She left Islam and followed Jesus Christ.

There is no doubt that you also have a desire for peace and comfort deep in your heart. If this is the case, you then need to allow that desire to turn into action, bring comfort into your life and remove the agents of discomfort from your life. For this, you need to follow Jesus Christ. No other one can give you real peace and comfort.

Reflection Time 19

1. Don't you think bluffing, lying and deceiving are invasions of others' rights and freedom?
2. If we deceive others, will it affect our own lives and the lives of our families? In what ways?
3. How difficult will it be for you to protect yourself and your family against bluffs, lying, deceit and political games when your own religion welcomes them? What is the best way to become free in this case?
4. The Gospel of Jesus Christ says that no lie comes from the truth. What does this mean for you spiritually and logically?
5. It what ways can we honor Jesus for his honest teachings?

There Is No Salvation Outside of Jesus

The Gospel of Jesus Christ in the book of Acts chapter 4 verses 10 to 12 says that there is no other name except the name of Jesus Christ whereby we must be saved. In other words, there is neither a person nor an angel nor a religion nor any religious practices, traditions or rituals in the entire world to save you from sin and Satan and give you eternal life, but the person of Jesus Christ.

How can Jesus save you?

Who can really save you except God or the One who has divine power to overcome Satan? He can release you from Satan's bondage and furthermore keep you in a safe situation far from the touches and pains of Satan. How can Jesus save you if He is not God? The Gospel says that Jesus is God and the Savior of humanity cannot be any one else but Jesus Christ who came to live in this world as the Word and Spirit of God and as the manifestation of God Himself.

He is the One whose Name is Immanuel which means God with us. His Name is also Jesus which means Redeemer and Savior. He is also called Messiah which means solely anointed and has divine authority for the task of salvation. Are there any spiritual, as well as logical, reasons behind the claims of the Gospel whereby to convince people's minds, hearts and consciences to follow Jesus? Is the Gospel able to prove that Jesus is God Himself and able to pave the way for people to be saved and have access to heaven?

The prophecies about Jesus and their fulfillment

Before revealing the reasons of the Gospel let me first read some prophesies that were made about Jesus centuries before Him. There are more than 300 hundred prophesies that Prophets before Jesus told about Him. The Gospel gives us a summary of these prophets' belief about Jesus Christ in the book of Acts chapter 10 verse 43. It says: "Every one of the prophets has said that all who have faith in Jesus will have their sins forgiven in his name." (CEV)

These prophesies are astonishingly amazing. They were told from 1200 to 400 years before Jesus and all were fulfilled by Jesus after He was born till the time He ascended into heaven. I am going to touch on several of them only.

Around seven hundred years before the birth of Jesus Christ the prophet Isaiah prophesied about Jesus Christ and said: The Lord Himself shall give you a sign. Behold, the virgin will conceive and shall bring forth a son, and they shall call His name Immanuel. (Isaiah 7:14, MKJV) Immanuel means God with us.

Isaiah prophesied again (Isaiah 9:6-7): For to us a Child is born, to us a Son is given; and the government shall be on His shoulder; and His name shall be called Wonderful, Counselor, The mighty God, The everlasting Father, The Prince of Peace. There is no end of the increase of His government and peace on the throne of David, and on His kingdom, to order it and to establish it with judgment and with justice from now on, even forever. The zeal of Jehovah of Hosts will do this. (MKJV)

See what the prophet David says in Psalm 45 verse 6 about Jesus: "You are God, and you will rule forever as king. Your royal power brings about justice." (CEV)

So centuries before Jesus the prophets of the Bible saw God desiring to manifest Himself as a man in order to reach to humanity and establish intimate relationships with them. They believed that God would manifest His fullness through the body of Jesus Christ in order to demolish the kingdom of Satan in people's hearts and establish the kingdom of heaven in their hearts from now to the end. As the future events passed through their minds in visions they fixed their eyes to the glorious days when God would reveal Himself in Jesus on earth for establishing love, joy and peace over war and hatred. They saw Jesus Christ, His infinite Godhood and as the Prince of Peace, overthrowing the empire of darkness but enlightening the world. They also saw that His spiritual government was established so securely so that no one in heaven and on earth could overthrow it. That's why the prophet Isaiah said, "There is no end of the increase of His government and peace." For this reason, he said that the Child born of the Virgin would be called almighty God.

People heard these prophesies and were always waiting for God to come and dwell among them and release them from all their miseries. Jesus was born then and they saw all the qualities of God in Him. They saw Him stop the storm in the sea. They saw Him raising dead ones to life, giving sight to blind people, healing the paralyzed and alleviating every kind of illness. He even claimed that anyone who had seen Him had seen the heavenly Father.

The whole fullness of God dwelled in Jesus

The Gospel says in the book of Hebrews chapter 1 verse 3: Jesus has all the brightness of God's own glory and is like him in every way. By his own mighty word, he holds the universe together. (CEV) The same chapter in the book of Hebrews verse 8 confirms what the Prophet David said about Jesus: "You are God, and you will rule as King forever! Your royal power brings about justice." (CEV)

The Gospel also says in Colossians chapter 1 verse 18 that the whole fullness of God dwelled in Jesus Christ. In other words, Jesus is God, almighty to do everything and there is nothing that He will not be able to do. Paul the Apostle of Jesus Christ says in his letter to Philippians chapter 4 verse 13 of the Gospel: "I can do all things through Christ who strengthens me." (ESV)

God revealed Himself in Jesus for the salvation of people

So the whole story of the Bible from the beginning to the end is based on the belief that God is the only Savior and He reveals Himself in Jesus to save people, make them victorious over Satan and lead them to heaven.

If you believe in the existence of God, you also need to believe that God is almighty and He can save people from the bondage of Satan and all kinds of spiritual and physical chains. You also need to believe that as Creation necessitated God to reveal Himself personally and create Adam and Eve, the salvation also necessitates God's personal revelation and touch in order to save people and continually look after them. You therefore need to allow God to sit on the throne of your heart personally and occupy it fully so that no place is left for Satan to reside in your heart and bother you. Neither God loves to give a place to Satan nor Satan to God. They do not like one another and never want to live together in one heart.

Therefore, either God must live in your heart or Satan. If Satan lives in your heart, it will mean that you neither have God, nor are saved nor have the assurance of salvation. But if you give way to God to live in your heart, then you will belong to God, to His heaven and will have the assurance of salvation forever. This is why that God's revelation in Jesus Christ becomes so vital in our lives. Nobody is able to save us from the hands of Satan unless God reveals Himself to us in order to engineer his plan for our salvation personally, overthrowing the kingdom of Satan in our hearts.

How does God overthrow the kingdom of Satan in our hearts and in what ways He implement His plan in our lives?

Let me first tell you how the kingdom of Satan improves so that then it will be easier to understand its collapse. Every soul that Satan wins and chains becomes a cause of advancement for his kingdom. In a similar way, every humankind who comes out of his kingdom and unites with God becomes a reason for the destruction of Satan's kingdom. In other words, you will advance the kingdom of Satan if you are not saved and do not have the assurance of salvation. But you will destroy the kingdom of Satan, if you allow Jesus to save you, to give you assurance and make your identity a heavenly one.

It is impossible to overcome Satan without Jesus. Since Satan is the master of deception and lies, he reveals himself in superficially good ways and in any possible way, even as a false prophet, in order to trap you. You are more likely to be deceived if you do not have a good role model in your life. That's why I told you that the revelation of God in Jesus Christ is very vital for us.

Nobody can become the best model of life for us except God in Jesus. Among humanity, everybody has given way to Satan and sinned. Even Muhammad, the prophet of Islam, said in Sura (7) Al A'araf verse 188 that Satan touched him and caused him to sin. Everybody has been involved in lawlessness, ignored the rights of others and has, consciously or unconsciously, served the cause of Satan. Sinful people cannot be good role models. Only God who is sinless and revealed Himself as sinless Jesus can become our good role model. He appeared in the body of Jesus to us so that we would be able to understand the quality of the best role model who can make us victorious in every aspect of life either philosophically, doctrinally, socially, politically or morally.

Jesus showed the best model through His life on earth and proved it through His actions recorded in the Gospel. He teaches us philosophically that God, unlike in other religions, never hides Himself but always is accessible and ready to sit in our hearts and stand behind us against Satan whose plan is our death. He also teaches us doctrinally that God is holy, just, loving, kind, peace-loving God and He never cooperates with Satan. Whereas we already have seen in the beginning verses of Sura Al Jinn (72) in the Quran that the god of Islam uses demons for the spread of his own religion, Islam.

The life and teachings of Jesus on earth have clearly proven that any person or god who collaborates with Satan and demons is not of the truth and unable to save people. That's why people need to search for the true Savior. Jesus also teaches us socially, morally and politically that the best model leads us to loving, happy, peaceful, patient, kind, good, faithful, gentle, and self-controlled relationships. Any one who turns his or her back on these values will be unable to lead people to salvation or to unity with God. So, you understand in every aspect now why there is no any other name in heaven or on earth except the Name of Jesus Christ whereby we must be saved. That's why the Gospel tells us: The reason that Jesus Christ came to this world was to save the lost. (Luke 19:10)

Those who are lost are those who are not saved, do not have the assurance of salvation and are always exposed to the schemes and touches of Satan. The only time that Satan is unable to touch and misguide us is when we belong to the kingdom of heaven and are protected under the leadership and Spirit of Jesus Christ. Many people in the world are following a religion simply because their parents or relatives follow that religion. They do not know that their religion is unable to reveal God to them so that God can hold them under His wings against sin and Satan. But the desire of God for us is to follow a belief which we know is truthful, have reasons for its own truthfulness, is able to save us and lead us in the path of righteousness to heaven.

I am so glad and fortunate that my eyes were opened and I realized that my personal relationship with God was more important for God than everything else. I therefore aligned myself with the desire of God for my salvation, searched for the best model and found Jesus. I found wonderful reasons that Jesus is the best Way, the source of Truth and the Life. He is the only One to save people. And I gave my life to Him. You can do the same and put your trust in Him too. He is able to save you too.

Reflection Time 20

1. People believe that God is everywhere. If so, don't you think that He is able to reveal Himself to you wherever you are?
2. If God is a revealing God, what then can stop us from believing the testimony of those who saw God?
3. God created mankind with His personal touch and breath, don't you think that in salvation (spiritual newness) God's personal touch is necessary as well?
4. Isn't it good to be embraced and saved by God personally?
5. Moses said that God revealed Himself to him like a fire. He also spoke to God face to face. The Gospel says that God revealed Himself in Jesus to save the world. What do you think, can't God reveal Himself in any way He wishes?

6. Why is it important for God to personally get involved (actually becoming a person) to save people?

7. All other religions leave the salvation of people to their own efforts, but the Gospel says that only God can save. Which salvation can be trusted more - that of man or that of God?

8. If you desire to be saved by God, you then need to follow Jesus Christ because only in Jesus Christ's faith is God the Savior.

Jesus Is the Way, the Truth and the Life

Jesus says in the Gospel: I am the Way, the Truth and the Life; no one comes to the Father but by Me. (John 14:6, MKJV)

All those people who believe in God love having confidence in being with God forever. Jesus is giving this comforting assurance to people which no one was able to do before. He is saying that He is the Way and able to take people to heaven for eternity.

Jesus is the Way to Heaven

Jesus is not speaking here like a prophet who says if you do this or do that you may be able to go to heaven. He is saying that He Himself is the Way to heaven. Anyone who puts his faith in Him will absolutely enter heaven. So Jesus is not like prophets who just described the way to their followers but were not able to do more than that. He instead manifested His ascendance to heaven. His disciples and hundreds of others saw Him ascending to heaven from this life and believed in Him who said that He would take His followers to heaven where He Himself is. Therefore, Jesus is the Way. You and I need to put our trust in Him if we want to have access to heaven and God and be eternally saved.

Do you know that anyone who wants to give us good news must himself be the example of that good news? The prophet of Islam said that you may go to heaven, but he himself was not sure of going to heaven nor was he able to demonstrate the ascendance to heaven as Jesus did.

After Muhammad died, his followers delayed the burial. Believing that he did not deserve to be buried under the dust, they expected his ascendance to heaven like Jesus. It did not happen, and as a result, one of his successors convinced the multitude that Muhammad was just like them and had to experience death like them. In other words, he was not like Jesus who was able to rise from the dead and ascend into heaven.

No one is like Jesus. He defeated death and now is sitting on the throne of heaven and able to make you and I heavenly if we decide to follow Him.

Jesus also said that He is the Truth.

We will not be able to understand this claim of Jesus unless we understand what Truth is. Truth is the illustration of things as they are. It never tolerates a false image of things. For example, the truth describes God as Someone who does not lie or deceive because He is just and holy by nature.

Jesus and His Gospel never call God a liar or deceiver, but Muhammad in his Quran says that God is the best of deceivers and sanctions lying under some circumstances. I have already given references from the Quran in the previous talks that lying and deception are accepted as ethical for the advancement of Islam. In Islam you can give false testimony to destroy the life of an opponent or a non-Muslim.

These are absolutely forbidden in the Gospel of Jesus Christ. You are not allowed to tell a lie or give a false witness against any one, including your enemy, because the Truth never promotes untruth. The Gospel in the book of James chapter 3 verses 10 to 12 says: Out of the same mouth should not proceed blessing and cursing. Does a fountain send forth at the same hole the sweet and the bitter? Can the fig tree, my brothers, bear olive berries; or a vine, figs? So no fountain can yield both salt water and fresh. (MKJV) In a similar way, if the Truth is the fountain in our hearts, our tongues must therefore speak the truth. But if we lie or deceive it means that evil is the fountain of our hearts, not the truth.

The lips of God also speak from His heart. His heart is the place of absolute Truth. There is not any essence of lying or deception in God's heart; and for this reason He never lies nor deceives nor instructs anyone to lie or deceive. Therefore, any prophet or religion that attributes lying and deception to God, no matter for what reason, cannot be of God and of the Truth.

The life of Jesus Christ on earth was the perfect revelation of God's truth without any lying and deception. His Gospel also rejects any kind of lie and deception, even the convenient ones. Therefore, Jesus is right in His claim when He says that He is the Truth. He does not attribute any lie and deception to God, never encourages anyone to lie or deceive, and there is no lie nor deception in His words and actions. He is the source of truth, and His truthful life on earth is the very reason for us to trust Him now and forever.

Jesus also said that He is the Life.

The Gospel says in the book of John chapter 1 verse 4 that in Jesus is life, and the life is the light of men. His life is such a life that gives eternal life, reflects the heavenly light to people and leads them to heaven. Jesus speaks in the Gospel in the book of John chapter 5 verse 25: Truly, truly, I say to you, an hour is coming, and is now here, when the dead will hear the voice of the Son of God, and those who hear will live. (MKJV) Jesus raised the dead and touched the heart of those who were alive and gave them eternal life. He proved His claim amongst people that He was the life-giver.

The work of Christ is not only guiding people like a prophet, but also cleaning their hearts from sins, renewing their hearts and giving them eternal life first and then guiding them in truth, holiness, righteousness, peace and love. A heart cannot be guided if it is not cleansed and renewed first. Also, no one can clean and renew a heart and guide it in truth unless He Himself is the life and the source of life. Jesus is that person. As the life and the source of life, He is the giver of life. So, Jesus is the Way to heaven. He is the only Way to reveal God and make Him accessible in our daily lives.

In the Way of Jesus Christ there is not any curtain between God and people

In Him people can be with God, talk to or hear His voice directly and unite with Him. But the Quran in Sura Ash Shura (42) verse 51 says that there is a curtain between Muhammad and his god, and the god in Islam never speaks to any one directly. It is here that you need to allow your conscience to make a right decision between the ways of Muhammad and Jesus. Muhammad taught that in his path to God, there will be always a curtain between him and God, but such a barrier does not exist in the path of Jesus. Therefore, Jesus is the right Way to heaven.

Secondly, Jesus is already in heaven but Muhammad is not according to the Quran. It is clearly obvious that the One who is in heaven can be the right Guide and Way to heaven.

Thirdly, only heavenly men and women can be with God and have access to Him. If you follow Jesus, you also become heavenly like Him and can be with God forever. Therefore, Jesus Christ is the hope to make God known to Muslims and to all.

Jesus is the hope to unite Muslims with God. Jesus is the only hope for Muslims to overcome Satan and become free on judgment day. Jesus is the hope to make Muslims heavenly. Put your trust in Jesus and receive the eternal joy of salvation.

Thank you so much for your patience all the way from the beginning of my talks to the end. I hope and pray that they were and will become helpful. God bless you.

Reflection Time 21

1. What makes Jesus different from a prophet?
2. Jesus said He is the Way to heaven. Is there any proof for His claim?
3. Jesus is from Heaven, is now in Heaven, knows the Way to Heaven and is able to guide us to Heaven. Is there anything to stop you from putting your trust in Him now?
4. Jesus also said that He is the Truth. Does His life on earth prove His claim?
5. If Jesus is the Truth, wouldn't it be good for you to accept Him as your truthful role model?
6. The life giving Spirit of God came to the Virgin Mary and she gave birth to an

absolutely holy and thereby life giving Son. That's why Jesus claimed to be the eternal Life and the source and giver of life. If you haven't put your trust in Him, please do it and receive eternal life.

Bibliography

Muhammad Jarir Tabari, Tabari's History, *"The History of Prophets and Kings"*

Qurans: Nobel Koran, Pickthall, Yusuf Ali and Dr. Mohsin.

Scripture quotations are from The Holy Bible, King James Version (KJV) (public domain).

Scripture taken from the Holy Bible, Modern King James Version ®, Copyright © 1962 – 1998. By Jay P. Green, Sr. Used by permission of the copyright holder.

Scripture quotations marked are from ESV (The Holy Bible, English Standard Version ®), Copyright © 2001 by Crossway, a publishing ministry of Good News Publishers. Used by permission. All rights reserved.

Scripture quotations are from The Holy Bible, NEW INTERNATIONAL VESION ®, Copyright © 1973, 1978, 1984 by International Bible Society. Used by permission of Zondervan Publishing House. All rights reserved.

Scripture quotations are from the (CEV) Contemporary English Version Copyright ® 1991, 1992, 1995 by American Bible Society, used by permission.

The Mecca Question by Jeremy Smyth, Copyright © Jeremy Smyth, 2011.

https://en.wikipedia.org/wiki/First_they_came_ ...

https://en.wikipedia.org/wiki/Giraffe#Neck;

http://www.africam.com/wildlife/giraffe_drinking

CPSIA information can be obtained at www.ICGtesting.com
Printed in the USA
BVOW01s0606020816

457376BV00003B/3/P